THE NORTHEAST
RAILROAD PROBLEM

George W. Hilton Goodman

American Enterprise Institute for Public Policy Research
Washington, D. C.

George W. Hilton is professor of economics, University of California, Los Angeles.

ISBN 0-8447-3175-7

Domestic Affairs Study 35, July 1975

Library of Congress Catalog Card No. L.C. 75-21701

© 1975 by American Enterprise Institute for Public Policy Research, Washington, D. C. Permission to quote from or to reproduce materials in this publication is granted when due acknowledgment is made.

Printed in the United States of America

CONTENTS

FOREWORD   1

1 ORIGINS OF THE PROBLEM   3

    Economic Organization   6
    Railroad Technology   16

2 ALTERNATIVE RAILROAD ORGANIZATION AND TECHNOLOGY   23

3 THE REGIONAL RAIL REORGANIZATION ACT OF 1973   29

    Content of the Act   34
    Formative Procedures under the Act   37

4 EVALUATION   45

    Consequences of the Act   45
    Analogies to Other Programs   48

APPENDIX   53

FOREWORD

This monograph examines the sources of the current problem of the bankrupt railroads of the northeastern United States and derives from this inquiry some indications of the proper policy to be followed. The policy indicated is then compared with the policy currently being implemented under the Regional Rail Reorganization Act of 1973. The monograph summarizes current estimates of the costs of establishing the Consolidated Rail Corporation, known as ConRail, and considers prospects for the success of the new system.

The planning process for establishing ConRail was completed on July 26, 1975, when the U.S. Railway Association submitted its final reorganization plan to the Congress. This plan will become effective at the end of sixty days unless the House of Representatives or the Senate disapproves it within that period. If either rejects the plan (and does not amend the reorganization act), the association must prepare and submit a revised plan for congressional consideration.

The analysis of the northeastern railroad problem presented here is adapted from the Final Report of the Task Force on Railroad Productivity, *Improving Railroad Productivity*, which was issued by the National Commission on Productivity and the President's Council of Economic Advisers in November 1973 almost simultaneously with passage of the Regional Rail Reorganization Act. It should be emphasized that the interpretation of the report is my own and that I have included here considerable material that was not in the report. Accordingly, neither all of my analysis nor all of my conclusions should be imputed to my fellow members of the task force and my fellow authors of its report.[1]

---

[1] *Improving Railroad Productivity*, Final Report of the Task Force on Railroad Productivity, a report to the National Commission on Productivity and the Council of Economic Advisers (Washington, D.C., November 1973). The chairman was John R. Meyer. The principal author of the report was Alexander L. Morton, executive director of the task force. See my summary of the report, "Why Pre-Electronic Railroading Survives," *Trains*, May 1974, pp. 20-24.

1
ORIGINS OF THE PROBLEM

The problems of the eastern railroads are not unique to them: these railroads are merely the most severe sufferers from the decline in the railroad industry which has been going on for about sixty years. The forces causing this decline include, but are not limited to, changes in the character of output from the American economy, shifts in the geographical pattern of the nation, the economic organization of the railroad industry in particular and of common carrier transportation in general, the present nature of railroad technology, and various combinations of these.

To a considerable extent the decline of the eastern railroads was made inevitable by the changes in the composition of the output of the U.S. economy and changes in the geographical pattern of that output.[1] Since the nineteenth century, our economy has shifted away from the production of goods toward the production of services. The conversion has been similar to that of the British economy—and has taken place for many of the same reasons it took place in Great Britain. The rising educational level of the U.S. population has led to a shift in the comparative advantage of the United States to the provision of such services as higher education, insurance, banking and other financial functions, and engineering, medical and legal services. The British economy made the same transition somewhat earlier than ours. The exhaustion of various raw materials, especially the depletion of U.S. iron ore reserves during World War II, reduced our comparative advantage for certain forms of heavy manufacturing—notably steel production. Beginning in the late 1930s, the Wagner Act led to the proliferation of unions in manufacturing industries, which in turn caused a reduction in the proportion of the labor

---

[1] *Improving Railroad Productivity*, chapter 1, pp. 1-50, *passim*.

force engaged in producing goods, and a corresponding increase in the proportion engaged in producing services.

The goods which the American economy produces are increasingly light in weight and high in value, and thus suitable to highway transport. Railroad rate structures and railroad technology gave a strong impetus to the development of a mode of transport with a comparative advantage for moving goods high in value relative to weight, as well as perishable or fragile. The mode developed was transport by truck. Increasingly the economy produces goods of this character: transistors, vacuum tubes, electronic gear of all sorts, ammunition, and small precision machinery. For an example of a city that embodies these characteristics more fully than any other we may look to Hartford, Connecticut. The city's local economy produces insurance policies, higher education, small precision manufactured goods, and aircraft engines which, though large, are highly subject to damage and share a high value-to-weight ratio with the small manufactures of the area. The variety of manufactures with these characteristics and the variety of points to which they are shipped have grown greatly so that specific point-to-point transportation of the sort offered by trucking is particularly suited to both the destinations and the character of the output. As a consequence the eastern railroads have increasingly become inbound terminating facilities for raw materials produced elsewhere in the United States. The output of the area which they serve more and more moves to its destination by truck. Their decline has therefore been, to a considerable degree, inevitable. Their problem has arisen from public policies that have impeded their adaptation to this decline.

The geographical change just described replaces a very different nineteenth century geographical pattern. At that time, the northeastern United States shipped finished manufactured goods to rural areas which, in turn, shipped agricultural products to the Northeast. This was a complementarity which suited the railroad technology of its time: the same boxcars moved finished products to rural areas for consumption and brought agricultural products back to the northeastern United States. Subsequently, manufacturing, especially of durable consumer goods, has spread more widely about the country. Rural areas have become depopulated or at best have remained relatively stagnant as the country has industrialized. The population of the nation has become increasingly concentrated in three major strip developments—along the east coast from Portland, Maine to Norfolk, Virginia, centering on New York; along the south shore of the Great Lakes from Green Bay, Wisconsin to Utica, New York, centering on Chicago; and on the west coast from the Mexican border to the north suburbs of San Francisco, centering on Los Angeles. The structure of rail rates has created an incentive to move raw materials long distances and final products shorter distances. Accordingly, raw materials tend to move into these strip developments for manufacture, and then the manufactured goods move shorter distances to the points of consumption—and increasingly, the final products move by truck.

The geographical distribution of mileage in the interstate freeway system, combined with the financing of the Highway Trust Fund by excises on gasoline and other inputs into driving, produces a subsidy of the South and West by the East, creating an incentive for relocation of industry out of the Northeast.

The eastern railroads have suffered more completely from these developments than others, partly because of the decline of manufacturing in the areas they serve, partly because several of them were dependent on originations of anthracite coal, and because all of them were dependent to a considerable extent on the American steel industry. Anthracite coal, once the dominant fuel for home heating in the Northeast, has been almost entirely superseded by natural gas (which does not move by railroad at all), by oil (which rarely moves by rail), or by electricity, which may be generated in several fashions (of which the most recent do not require extensive rail transportation). The inputs of nuclear power stations are small in volume, heavy in weight, and pose considerable safety risks. As a result, these inputs are likely to move by truck, or if they move by rail, they do not do so in large volume. Alternatively, electricity may be generated by coal at the mine mouth and transmitted long distances by high voltage alternating or direct current, again avoiding rail transportation.

Developments in the steel industry have been equally adverse for the railroads. The railroads lost consumer-goods traffic more rapidly than they lost capital-goods traffic. This had the inevitable consequence of making the entire industry increasingly vulnerable to business fluctuations as it declined, and specifically of making the eastern railroads increasingly dependent on the steel industry. The outstanding example was the Lehigh Valley Railroad, one of the bankrupt lines eligible for consolidation into the ConRail system. By the 1950s this railroad had become almost entirely dependent for its originations on a single steel plant in Bethlehem, Pennsylvania. Its fortunes fluctuated with those of the Bethlehem Steel Company in a fashion over which the management had essentially no control. The dependence of the Erie Railroad on the steel industry in Youngstown, Ohio was almost equally severe. The dependence of the Penn Central and its predecessors on the steel industry in Pittsburgh, Youngstown, Philadelphia and other cities on the system is not so extreme, but it is certainly noteworthy. Steel is apparently a declining industry; Germany and Japan appear now to have a comparative advantage in steel analogous to the advantage America had in earlier years.

Even apart from developments of this sort, there are other obvious sources for the weakness of the eastern railroads. They are the oldest American railroads and were built to early, relatively primitive engineering standards. They have considerable trackage in the Appalachian Mountains which, in general, lack long river courses and produce choppy rail profiles with difficult curvatures. They generally have relatively short operating districts, dating from the nineteenth century practices of steam locomotive replacement at frequent intervals. In several states they are beset by full-crew laws, which make their labor expenses higher relative to output than is the case for railroads in other sections of the country.

In addition, the eastern railroads have large shares of their assets in the form of urban terminal facilities than do railroads elsewhere in the country. These facilities were designed largely for termination of passengers or less-than-carload-freight, activities for which the railroads have also lost their comparative advantage, and the facilities are usually heavily taxed. The eastern railroads haul the majority of American commuters, an activity which is generally highly unprofitable. Indeed, in most major cities commuter service is operated under state or municipal subsidy. Frequently, such subsidies are not entirely compensatory but rather simply compensate for out-of-pocket losses.[2]

Economic Organization

The forces discussed above have worked particularly against the eastern railroads. The relative weakness of these eastern lines has given rise to a view in the railroad industry (and to some extent elsewhere) that the weakness of the railroads is exclusively, or almost exclusively, an eastern or northeastern problem. This is not correct. The strongest of the western and southern railroads earn rates of return which are only about half the rates of return on capital in manufacturing industries. The forces now to be discussed affect the entire railroad industry adversely; together, these forces prevent the railroads from achieving their comparative advantage for long-distance movements.

---

[2] See George W. Hilton, "The Decline of Railroad Commutation," *Business History Review*, vol. 36 (1962), pp. 171-187.

The railroad industry is a mixed public and private cartel whose origins and present implementation are major sources of the current problem. In the late nineteenth century the railroads, beginning in 1869 with three lines between Chicago and the eastern terminus of the Union Pacific at Omaha-Council Bluffs, engaged in collusive pricing coupled with pooling, usually of traffic, but sometimes of earnings. This practice caused the railroads to have the experience common to cartelized industries: in the short run, the practice resulted in a level of rail rates so high that in the 1870s there was considerable public outcry. In the principal agricultural states this outcry produced laws intended to hold down the absolute level of railroad rates.

A further consequence of cartelization was that the industry attracted excessive capital. Entry into railroading in the United States was relatively free: in order to secure powers of condemnation, the entrepreneur simply made a demonstration of financial responsibility to the secretary of state in the state in which he wanted to build. In Britain, by way of contrast, an act of Parliament was required to grant such rights. Accordingly, American railroads quickly found themselves duplicated by rival routes between the same termini. The Pennsylvania and the New York Central, which had completed lines from New York to Chicago in the mid-1850s, found themselves rivaled by three other major American carriers plus one Canadian by the early 1880s. William H. Vanderbilt made the famous statement that there were five great trunk lines from Chicago to the East Coast with traffic enough for two.[3]

As capital flowed into the railroads, the industry took on the characteristics of a mature cartel. Rates fell until, by the mid-1880s, they were on average the lowest in the world. As railroads proliferated, their quotas in the pool fell and their incentives to break out of the collusions increased. Accordingly the industry became chronically unstable by the mid-1880s.[4] Collusive contracts of this character were unenforceable in American law. If the cartels were to be stabilized, the federal government had to undertake the task. Congress did so in the form of the Interstate Commerce Act of 1887. This statute established the Interstate Commerce Commission (ICC) and equipped it with a set of powers intended to allow the rail cartels to stabilize themselves more effectively than they could have done in the absence of the act. As a consequence of an inconsistent recon-

---

[3] Lee Benson, *Merchants, Farmers and Railroads* (Ithaca, N.Y.: Cornell University Press, 1955), p. 36.
[4] See Paul W. MacAvoy, *The Economic Effects of Regulation* (Cambridge: MIT Press, 1965), and Gabriel Kolko, *Railroads and Regulation, 1907-1916* (Princeton: Princeton University Press, 1965).

ciliation of the Senate and House versions of the bill, pooling, which had been the principal private method of stabilizing the railroad cartels, was prohibited. This prohibition was one of several provisions which caused the act to be ineffective except transitionally.[5]

The prohibition of pooling was to be extremely important in the later history of the cartelization. The Interstate Commerce Commission was never vested with powers to issue quotas to the members of the cartel and was therefore forced to use its ratemaking authority to distribute traffic among the cartel members. This use of ratemaking authority for allocation of tonnage was to reach its maximum importance when the cartel was extended beyond the railroads between 1935 and 1942.

In the interim, however, most of the other inadequacies of the ICC's statutory authority were rectified by three acts passed between 1903 and 1910. By 1914 the Interstate Commerce Commission was succeeding in what it had been set up to do, stabilize the railroad cartels without pooling; the rate wars and rebating of the nineteenth century were ended. The railroads were collusively enforcing their tariffs, which by then had the authority of statutes. The tariffs embodied a discrimination based mainly on a calculation of the value of the commodity relative to its weight. This discrimination, however, served as an incentive for the development of a vehicle with a comparative advantage for moving goods which were high in value relative to weight. This vehicle took shape in the form of the truck. The development of the truck, along with improvements in towboat and barge transportation on the inland rivers, caused the railroads to become a declining industry beginning about 1916.

Because of World War I, the fact of the industry's decline was not immediately apparent. Congress, faced with the question of returning the railroads to their owners after a short period of government operation during and immediately following the war, produced the Transportation Act of 1920. This act was a straightforward cartelizing statute. It converted the Interstate Commerce Commission from a body that stabilized private cartels to an outright public cartelizing body vested with powers over minimum rates. The other normal accoutrements of cartelization were provided: control of entry and exit, control over capital formation, several devices which proved ineffective for equalizing the rates of return among carriers, and a target rate of return for the railroads. An effort to generate the target return of 5.75 percent in a declining industry resulted in a level of

---

[5] George W. Hilton, "The Consistency of the Interstate Commerce Act," *The Journal of Law & Economics*, vol. 9 (1966), pp. 87-113.

rail rates so high that the incentive for shippers to turn to trucks increased.

The proliferation of intercity trucking after 1926 created political pressures which eventually led to the inclusion of trucks in the cartel. The Motor Carrier Act of 1935 extended the ICC's powers to interstate common carrier and contract carrier trucking. The act, however, provided abundant exemptions from regulation for private carriers and all motor carriers of agricultural products, so that about two-thirds of intercity trucking was exempt. The cartelized rates, of course, provided a powerful incentive for shippers to engage in private carriage.

The cartel was extended to water carriers in the Transportation Act of 1940. In this act the exemptions extended not only to agricultural and private carriage but to carriers of bulk commodities and liquids of all sorts, along with any cargo which required special handling devices, so that more than 90 percent of water carriage was outside the cartel. The result of all this was a non-pooling cartel consisting of 100 percent of railroading, approximately a third of trucking and less than 10 percent of water transport.

Even apart from the incomplete nature of the cartel, the statutory authority for running it was thoroughly unsatisfactory. The ICC's procedures were established by analogy to court procedures. The commission proceeded on a case-by-case basis, developing a body of jurisprudence as it went along. Its statutory authority lacked the specificity required for effective cartelization. The commission frequently fell back on the most nebulous part of the statutory authority, the National Transportation Policy (the preamble of the act added in 1940) in order to stop practices that had to be prevented to make the cartel work tolerably, but which are not specifically prohibited in any of the statutory authority. For example, if motor carrier rates are to be based on the value of the service rather than the cost of the service, motor carriers must be prohibited from filling empty back-hauls at rates which would merely cover the incremental cost of filling the back-haul. The ICC prohibits this by considering it a destructive competitive practice which is therefore proscribed under the National Transportation Policy.

A well-organized cartel, instead of using legalistic procedures of this character, would have a cartelizing body engaging in statistical calculations for the purpose of issuing quotas to equalize the marginal cost of each member of the cartel. It would also allow a market in cartel quotas so that, if errors were made in the calculation of marginal costs, the rights to produce output would go to their highest valued use. There is nothing of this sort in the ICC's authority. Rather, the ICC allocates freight by using its authority over rates to divide the traffic among carriers. Professor Ernest Williams has demonstrated that, when confronted by a controversy between motor carriers and railroads over the appropriate level of rates for freight, the ICC will habitually set rates at levels such that the traffic may be divided between the two. That is to say, the commission will establish motor carrier rates sufficiently higher than railroad rates so that some shippers will choose the higher quality of service by truck at the higher rates and some will choose the lower quality of service by railroad at the lower rates.[6]

This practice squares well with the incentives of the commissioners. It minimizes hostility on the part of regulated industries because each may get some of the traffic. It therefore preserves the commissioners' support in a Congress responsive to its constituencies and their own options for post-commission employment. In any case the commission is not directed by its statutory authority to secure optimal resource allocation. The policy followed prevents the carriers from achieving their comparative advantage on the basis of their relative costs for shipments of varying degrees of damage proneness, perishability, urgency and so on. The commission maintains a relatively rigorous separation of modes. By devices such as that just described, it ensures that trucks, railroads, and barge lines are kept in rivalry with one another—which is the antithesis of pursuing policies that would allow each mode to be used in accordance with its comparative advantage. The cost of misallocation of freight between railroads and truck lines has been estimated to be as high as $2.8 billion per year.[7]

The policy embodied in the Interstate Commerce Act and its subsequent amendments has tended to perpetuate the problem which the act was designed to solve. The cartelization of railroads in the nineteenth century was carried out on a regional basis, with the minor exception of certain cartels set up for specific commodities. One may look at a map of the United States today and see where those cartels were: from Chicago and St. Louis to the east coast ports, from Ohio and Potomac River crossings to the south, from Chicago to the Missouri River crossings, along with counterparts to the west. Only a few lines—such as the Wabash main line from Kansas City to

---

[6] Ernest W. Williams, *The Regulation of Rail-Motor Rate Competition* (New York: Harpers, 1958), pp. 213-214.
[7] Robert W. Harbeson, "Toward Better Resource Allocation in Transport," *The Journal of Law & Economics*, vol. 12 (1969), esp. pp. 332-334.

Toledo and the Frisco line from Kansas City to Birmingham—violated these patterns. The result was a balkanized system of railroading.

The adoption by the mid-1880s of a standard gauge of 4 feet, 8½ inches, and of the present coupling and air-brake system resulted in a homogeneous technology which permitted cars to circulate freely about the United States. A combination of this homogeneous technology and the balkanized geographical pattern ensured that the majority of shipments—somewhat more than half—would move jointly between railroads. The industry was organized in such a way that the railroads would continually be in the position of rivals and joint venturers simultaneously.

This organization produces a variety of adverse incentives for the railroads. When a railroad receives a freight car in interchange, its only incentive is to move that car to its destination or to an interchange with the car's next railroad as cheaply as possible. The railroad's remuneration for the movement is fixed by a division which is set collusively, subject to ICC approval, in the same fashion as the rates are set. The railroad receives no premium for getting the car to its destination quickly and, if the cargo is damaged, the originating railroad bears the bill. Railroading as it is currently organized has essentially none of the growth potential of trucking.

In order to equal the productivity increases achieved in manufacturing—with which railroading competes for labor—the railroads endeavor to increase output per employee by running longer trains. This entails having cars sit around for long periods waiting to be made up into trains. The nature of the technology (which will be described below) is such that the longer the train, the higher the probability both of damage to its cargo and of derailment. Accordingly, the effort to run longer trains produces a lower quality of service in two major respects. It becomes impossible for the railroads to give a high degree of assurance of cargo arrival times, whereas the arrival of a truck, even on a transcontinental trip, can usually be estimated within a few hours. Obviously, the more highly valued the commodities being carried, the greater the demand on the part of manufacturers for assurances about delivery—and the trend has been toward more highly valued commodities. The deterioration in quality of service so far as it affects assurance of delivery is a serious handicap of the same sort as the high incidence of damage claims.

In addition, the organization of the industry produces relatively low utilization of the capital embodied in freight cars. The typical American freight car operates only about 2¾ hours per day, traveling about fifty miles, and sits idle in a yard, on a siding, or elsewhere for about 21¼ hours. There has been some improvement in the ratio between time used and time idle, mainly because of the high rate of utilization of piggy-back flat cars, but the improvement has been relatively minor.

The situation is compounded by the nature of the pricing of railroad cars. Railroads pay one another a "per diem" fee for the use of one another's cars depending on where the car is at midnight. At present, the fee differs according to the type of car, and it has both a daily component and a mileage component. It is customarily argued that the daily component is too low and the mileage component too high, so that railroads have an incentive to hoard the cars of other railroads on their properties. The per diem fee, not being a market-determined price, does not fluctuate in response to demand. In peak seasons, notably when agricultural products are moving in the fall, there is therefore excess demand. The railroads have an incentive to hoard rolling stock against periods of excess demand and then to engage in non-price rationing, favoring habitual shippers in allocation of cars. It should be noted also that the railroads' incentive is to have as flimsy a car as will meet the interchange requirements.[8]

Inevitably, the way in which this industry is organized creates an incentive to engage in what *Improving Railroad Productivity* calls counterproductive investment, that is, investment which is profitable only because of the inappropriate organization of the industry. Gravity classification yards are usually considered the preeminent example of such investment. They use highly capital-intensive methods to make up the long trains which the industry has an incentive to run and, because of switching impacts at excessive speeds, are a major source of damage to cargo. In such a classification yard, if a car rolling down from the hump falls short of the cars in the train with which it is being mated, the railroad that operates the yard incurs the cost of sending out a switch engine to bring about a coupling. On the other hand, if coupling occurs at an excessive speed so that the cargo is damaged, the railroad that originated the shipment bears the cost. Accordingly, as one would expect, in gravity classification, railroads err on the side of excessive coupling impact. One writer has estimated the average speed of impact at 7.4 miles per hour—which is great enough to damage a considerable amount of railroad cargo. The force of an impact is proportional to the square of the speed of impact. An impact speed of only six miles per hour does somewhat more than double the damage of the optimal impact speed of four

---

[8] E. V. Mosbach, "Economic Analysis of Per Diem Rates of Freight Cars" (Washington: Jack Faucett Associates, 1971).

miles per hour. Most cargo is not given a safety factor of more than 100 percent in packing [9]—that is, it cannot stand an impact of more than double the optimal.

Classification yards are not the only counterproductive investment in the industry. Main-line electrification, because it is based on acceptance of existing technology and economic organization, should probably also be classified as counterproductive investment.

From the point of view of the eastern railroad problem, one of the worst aspects of the inappropriate incentives given to the railroads is the incentive to merger. Mergers in the industry are subject to approval by the Interstate Commerce Commission. As usual, the statutory authority provides only vague guidelines so that essentially the commission may be said to have administrative discretion in approving or disapproving a merger. The mergers, in other words, are a product of the distorted incentives of the industry, subject to ICC review.

There are three possible motives for merging railroads. First, railroads may be merged so as to create a geographical pattern which, with the changes in technology to be described in the following chapter, would be consistent with competitive organization of the industry. This would involve end-to-end mergers toward the goal of creating a small number of rival nationwide rail systems. Given the present organization of the industry, neither the commission nor the individual railroads have incentives to bring about mergers of this kind because, typically, the cost savings are not substantial.

However, the railroads and the commission do have reason to bring about mergers for either of two other purposes. One is to merge parallel lines so as to consolidate terminal activity and make use of the better physical plant for intercity service. The merger movement that began in the mid-1950s was motivated by the hope of such savings. Thus the Seaboard Air Line and Atlantic Coast Line expected their merger to reduce costs by 12.4 percent, and the others that merged for this reason expected savings of up to 8.1 percent. The experience of most of them fell considerably short of their expectations.[10] The relatively poor showing for mergers of parallel railroads may be attributed to any of several considerations. The academic literature on economies of scale in railroading consistently demonstrates that these economies are mild, no greater than those found in heavy manufacturing, smelting, large-scale liquid processing, or most

---

[9] See George W. Hilton, "Slack," *Trains*, forthcoming.
[10] *Improving Railroad Productivity*, pp. 246-256.

assembly-line operations, and that they can be fully realized in a railroad of intermediate size. Moreover, it shows that in the very largest railroads there may be outright diseconomies of scale.[11]

The Penn Central merger is the largest merger of parallel railroads undertaken in an effort to secure economies of scale in terminal operations and preferable routing of freight on the basis of the superiority of the physical plant of one predecessor railroad over the other. It was, of course, the most unsuccessful of such mergers. It is generally thought that the predecessor railroads would have been better off had they never been joined. Such labor economies as they sought were largely signed away in agreement with the unions. Moreover, the incompatibility of their computers caused the predecessors to continue operating separately in certain respects, and the confusion of outsiders at the separately operated facilities was a conspicuous diseconomy.

The third possible motive for railroad mergers is to make possible subsidization of weak railroads by the strong. This motive seems to be important to the Interstate Commerce Commission. As Richard Posner and others have pointed out, regulation is essentially a form of taxation in which monopoly gains generated in one activity are used to subsidize some other activity.[12] Political pressures cause the Interstate Commerce Commission to try to retain mileage in the industry and, in particular, to prevent weak railroads from going out of business entirely. One method of doing this is to merge weak railroads with strong. Just now (July 1975) the Interstate Commerce Commission is endeavoring to induce the Santa Fe to take over the Missouri-Kansas-Texas, for example. The Penn Central merger involved a strong element of this: the Pennsylvania and New York Central, as a condition of merging, were forced to take over what was then the weakest American railroad, the New York, New Haven & Hartford.

Such behavior can succeed only when monopoly gain can be generated in one activity for use in subsidizing the other. When this ceased to be possible in the case of passenger trains, some other method of financing such trains had to be found if they were to be kept from passing out of existence. The method chosen was the use

---

[11] Kent T. Healy, *The Effects of Scale in the Railroad Industry* (New Haven: Yale University Committee on Transportation, 1961); Robert E. Gallamore, "Railroad Mergers: Costs, Competition, and the Future of the American Railroad Industry" (unpublished doctoral dissertation, Harvard University, 1968).
[12] Richard Posner, "Taxation by Regulation," *Bell Journal of Economics and Management Science*, vol. 2 (1971), pp. 22-50.

of general tax revenues through the Amtrak system.[13] The analogy to the establishment of the proposed ConRail system should be apparent.

Similar considerations are involved in the abandonment of branch lines. The argument presented here demonstrates why the mileage in redundant branch lines is so great. The pooling of railroad traffic in the nineteenth century extended only to traffic received from connections. Traffic which a railroad originated itself was not pooled. This gave railroads an incentive to originate as much of their traffic as they could relative to what they received from their connections. Accordingly, those railroads which were most characterized by redundant main lines paralleling one another between common terminal points also came to be characterized by high mileages of branch lines. Iowa, and neighboring states in the upper Midwest more generally, have been the worst offenders in this respect. Michigan and eastern Pennsylvania, owing to the decline of lumbering and anthracite coal, also abound in redundant mileage. At present, main-line earnings are expected to subsidize branch lines. Shippers and consignees on branch lines, therefore, are receiving a subsidy and, like most recipients of subsidies, have incentives to fight politically to retain them.

Branch-line abandonment and other abandonments are subject to an exit control by the Interstate Commerce Commission under the Transportation Act of 1920. This control produces perversity in choosing branch lines for abandonment. The branch lines with the least traffic tend not to be the most unprofitable. A branch line that rarely has a train runs up taxes, but it has small variable expenses and there is not a great deal of incentive to get rid of it. The most unprofitable branch lines are those with frequent short trains providing a pick-up and delivery function for which trucks have a comparative advantage. On the Penn Central, of 5,000 miles of unprofitable branch lines, the most lightly used 3,000 miles lose only about $2 million of the annual loss of $20 million for the whole 5,000 miles. It is the less utilized and less unprofitable branch lines which are typically abandoned because they generate the least political pressure for retention. The more unprofitable branch lines survive, wasting labor and trapping cars (for cars terminating on branch lines typically wait relatively long periods before being removed).[14]

---

[13] See James C. Miller III, "An Economic Policy Analysis of the Amtrak Program," in *Perspectives on Federal Transportation Policy* (Washington, D.C.: American Enterprise Institute for Public Policy Research, 1975), pp. 145-163.

[14] *Improving Railroad Productivity*, pp. 157-186.

Railroad Technology

Intrinsic to all that has been said here is the presumption that present railroad technology is undesirable and poorly suited to present-day demands. The technology involving locomotives and individual cars which the industry uses was developed in the nineteenth century when steam locomotives were universal. The power was necessarily concentrated at the head of the train. The method of coupling and braking currently used was developed in the immediate post-Civil War period. The coupling system was developed by Eli H. Janney in 1868 and the pneumatic braking system by George Westinghouse in 1869. The combination was formally adopted in 1887. Both the coupling and the braking systems are nonelectric—as was inevitable, given the early date at which they were invented.

As mentioned before, the coupler requires a considerable impact at an optimal speed of four miles per hour in order to close the device and secure the coupling. To protect the car and its cargo against this impact, the coupler is mounted on a pair of springs which, together with their housing, are known as draft gear. The springs extend approximately 2.7 inches and are fitted with a set of plates by which the energy from the rebound of the springs is dissipated in heat from the friction. An ordinarily equipped car has about 5½ inches of controlled slack in the draft gear. In addition, it has about 3 to 6 inches of uncontrolled slack, called free slack, in the looseness of the coupler and the stretching of the equipment.

This foot or so of slack in a car makes it possible for the locomotive to start one car at a time or a few cars at a time; a given locomotive can keep about ten times as much tonnage rolling as it can start. In early railroading this function of slack was more important than cushioning the cargo. With the replacement of steam locomotives with diesel engines—which have a continuous rather than a discrete torque—this function has declined in importance relative to the cushioning of cargo against switching impact. Within the past two decades several devices have been introduced to increase the travel of couplers for better cushioning against impact. As a result, trains now average somewhat more than a foot of slack per car. An ordinary modern American mainline freight train will lengthen by 125 to 150 feet while going upgrade or accelerating and will contract by the same amount while decelerating or going down hill.

An incidental consequence of this method of making up railroad trains is that every car must be strong enough to be the first car in a train, even though it may in fact be the last. This means that a great deal of the weight of a car is in its center sill. It has been pointed out that the incentives derived from the way cars are priced lead railroads to build cars that are as flimsy as they can possibly be and still meet interchange requirements. To say this is not inconsistent with saying that a disproportionate amount of the weight of the cars is in the center sill. The distribution of weight between the center sill and the superstructure is yet another example of counterproductive investment in the industry.

Similarly, the incentives in the industry, especially over the course of the last twenty years, have caused the railroads to build a large number of highly unstable cars. Piggy-back flat cars, for example, are long, rigid, light, and have couplers with long travel. Such cars are usually around eighty-five feet in length with an overhang beyond the trucks of about twelve to nineteen feet to the coupler face. The coupler shanks are about five feet long. When unloaded they are prone to derailment on curves or on entering sidings, especially when slack is running in. When loaded, they can handle two semi-trailers. Thus, they have high centers of gravity, wide amplitudes and long natural frequencies when swaying from side to side. They are particularly unstable when loaded with only one semi-trailer and when that semi-trailer is at the rear of the car.[15]

American railroads opt for piggy-back instead of containers because of incentives in the economic organization of the industry. Container terminals involve considerable economies of scale, so they are optimally located at intervals of about 300 miles or in the immediate vicinity of large cities. Piggy-back terminals, on the other hand, are simple ramps which can be placed anywhere. Some 1,400 of these dot the nation. The restrictions on highway operations by railroads and by non-railroad owners of semi-trailers cause them to prefer to unload the trailers from flatcars close to their destinations. Accordingly, American railroads have chosen piggy-backing, whereas most of their foreign counterparts have chosen containerization. Containers on flatcars produce a vehicle with a lower center of gravity, shorter natural sway frequency, and only about a third of the wind resistance of a loaded piggy-back flat.

Similarly, tri-level automobile racks when loaded have high centers of gravity with wide amplitudes. Covered hopper cars of the sort introduced since 1960 in an effort to secure ICC approval of grain rates at barge-competitive levels are also highly unstable. Such cars have proven to have natural frequencies of side-to-side (so-called "rock and roll") movement that are augmented by the thirty-nine-foot

---

[15] Hilton, "Slack."

interval of staggered rail joints characteristic of American track, especially between fifteen and thirty miles per hour.

The augmentation of cars' natural frequencies by the thirty-nine-foot rail-joint interval is highly concentrated between ten and thirty miles per hour for equipment of all sorts—a fact which is extremely important in explaining the deterioration of service on the bankrupt northeastern railroads. Mainline railroads ordinarily have speed limits for freight trains from forty miles per hour to the seventy-five miles per hour which is usually considered the maximum safe speed for standard freight trucks. Deterioration of rail joints from inadequate maintenance does not, at least initially, prevent operation at these speeds, but rather makes it unsafe to reach them by passing through the ten-to-thirty-mile-per-hour range. Accordingly, the safe speed on a deteriorated railroad falls not from fifty miles per hour to forty, but rather to ten, just below the range of maximum stability. As one would expect, operation of a railroad at ten miles per hour is extremely uneconomic. The quality of the service repels shippers, the productivity of the employees and of the motive power declines, and scheduled connections become impossible to maintain. In particular, wage expenses increase greatly as crews have to tie up after twelve hours of service under the Adamson Act, as amended. The astronomical losses of the Penn Central stem largely from the costs of operating a highly deteriorated railroad. By March 1974, 8,475 miles of the Penn Central, some 43 percent of its mileage, was operable only under slow orders. The railroad was also experiencing more than twenty derailments a day.[16]

The braking mechanism on American railroads is a pneumatic, nonelectric system in which the braking impulse is not transmitted instantaneously. In present practice, the service application—which is to say the ordinary use of the air brakes—is transmitted at approximately 400 to 600 feet per second. The emergency application is transmitted at approximately 900 to 950 feet per second. Free slack runs in and out of trains at approximately 200 to 400 feet per second. A railroad train has some of the properties of a chain; it is more stable when fully stretched than when being pushed together. Combine all of these technological properties and we can see that American freight trains are highly unstable in emergency braking applications. If an engineer sees an obstruction on the track—for example, a truck making a retail delivery of gasoline—he must stop as quickly as possible and will give the fast-moving train an emergency brake application. It will take about seven to eleven seconds for the impulse to travel

---

[16] "A Railroad Comes Unglued," *Trains*, August 1974, p. 8.

the length of an ordinary mainline freight train, and as long as ninety seconds before brakes are being applied on all cars. The brake impulse will be applied differentially according to the speed of the response on individual cars, the degree of brake wear, and various other considerations. The train will contract at the rate of about a foot per car, almost instantaneously. The cars will hit one another with the equivalent of the switching impact of about fourteen miles per hour at worst. The lateral vectors in the cars will be augmented, and the train is almost certain to derail. Derailments of this sort have caused fires from propane tank cars and detonations of explosive material. The braking system is designed to be fail-safe in the sense that the brakes go on, not off, in the event of a parting of the train. Unfortunately, they will also go on in the event of a malfunction on a moving train. A malfunctioning car, called a "kicker" or a "dynamiter," can cause an emergency application without notice.[17]

Even in less drastic situations, American freight trains are unstable. Trains are made up randomly based on the order of the arrival and departure of cars in a yard or based on pre-blocking to destinations. They are not made up in consideration of their track-train dynamic properties. A series of several empty piggy-back flats together is a dangerous source of instability at low speed. An engineer who uses dynamic braking or engine brake alone at low speed to go

---

[17] A good example of the sort of wreck which can arise at any time from the inherent elements of present railroad technology is the following, from *Trains*, February 1975, pp. 10-11:

The misgivings of the National Transportation Safety Board about the existing freight-train braking system were reinforced by a sequence of events that occurred on the Delaware & Hudson near Oneonta, N.Y., starting about 4:20 p.m. on February 12, 1974. Northbound symbol freight NWB-4—a U33C and 2 U30C diesels and 122 cars—was entering a 3½-degree curve at 32 mph when the fourth car behind the engine, C&O covered hopper 603325, loaded with 190,000 pounds of shelled corn, gave up the ghost, triggering these events:
 1. The center sill of the hopper fractured, deflecting downward, which in turn distorted the north end of the sill upward about 7½ inches. 2. When the north end of the hopper went up, its coupler moved vertically, disengaging from the car ahead. 3. As couplers parted, so did the air-brake hoses, causing an emergency brake application. 4. The power control switch reduced power to idle; braking action became effective initially on the locomotives and first three cars, and the rear 118 cars caught up and collided with the front end of the train, producing excessive run-in of slack. 5. This longitudinal force was converted to a lateral force on the trailing U30C, which was entering the 3½-degree curve, and produced a force against the east or high rail. This forced the rail outward, thus widening the track gauge. 6. Thereupon the west wheels of the diesels dropped inside the west rail and began destroying the track structure. 7. In the ensuing derailment, cars hit the ground parallel to the track, then began jackknifing. 8. Cars 21 through 27 in the consist were jumbo tankers, each loaded with an average of 30,200 gallons of liquefied petroleum gas, and they ruptured, ignited, and/or exploded.

into a siding will find that the run-in of slack, combined with the lateral movement on the switch, is liable to derail empty piggy-back flats and other extra-length cars on his train. Derailments of this sort are usually not serious.

Present railroad technology has led to more and more frequent derailments. Deterioration of rail joints augments the natural frequency of cars, notably of covered hoppers, at speeds under thirty miles per hour. The probability of derailment rises exponentially with the length of the train. A freight train has a probability of derailment from equipment-related causes of .001 at 100 cars, but .024 at over 250 cars. The number of cars derailing also increases more than proportionately to the increase in the length of the train.[18]

In sum, the incentives influencing railroads are such as to make freight trains more unstable over time. Railroads have an incentive to use increasingly longer trains, longer cars, and longer coupler travel. Deterioration of the railroads' physical plant augments the cars' natural frequencies and increases the lateral vectors relative to the longitudinal vectors in trains. Apart from considerations of railroad rivalry with trucking, the situation makes railroads more and more of a menace to on-line communities. In a well-publicized accident on July 19, 1974, an excessive switching impact in the Norfolk & Western yard at Decatur, Illinois detonated a tank car of propane, killing seven people, injuring 150, and inflicting about $15 million in property damage.[19] Current railroad technology, unfortunately, has the potential for even greater disasters.

Apart from these considerations, present railroad technology is overly labor-intensive. The coupling and braking system is automatic by late nineteenth century standards, but no longer can be considered so. It requires large numbers of men in yards to lift the lever which releases the coupler, to ensure that one of the knuckles of the couplers on the cars being coupled will be open, to make the connection between the rubber hoses that transmit the air line the length of the train, and to bleed off the air from the air reservoirs on the cars so that they can be switched in yards. This technology also encourages strong unions by placing several groups in crucial positions to tie up operations.

On the other hand, given the poor prospects of the railroad industry, it is easier for railroads to borrow on cars than on anything

---

[18] Robert H. Leilich, "A Study of the Economics of Short Trains" (Washington, D.C.: Peat, Marwick, Mitchell & Co., 1974), p. 10.
[19] "Decatur Devastated," *Trains*, October 1974, p. 13.

else. If a railroad repudiates equipment trusts, the cars can be repossessed and sold or leased to other railroads.

Basically, present railroad technology survives because it is well suited to the economic organization of an industry in which the firms are simultaneously rivals and joint venturers. This economic organization requires a compatible technology, and individual railroads have to be prevented from making independent modifications. What one railroad would do to protect its cars better from switching impact would probably add to the weight of the cars, which in turn would increase the probability that its cars would damage those of other railroads in the train make-up process. Accordingly, efforts at improvement must be carried out jointly. The Association of American Railroads, in collaboration with the Federal Railroad Administration, has a program in track-train dynamics which may produce recommendations for a new or improved coupling-braking system by the 1980s. A new system would require the replacement of some 3.4 million couplers, plus new braking technology.[20]

The direct actions of the Interstate Commerce Commission have reinforced the incentives to perpetuate the technology inherent in the economic organization of the industry. For example, the ICC imposes car service requirements, its rates are mainly based on carload lots, and it is currently engaged in an effort to force railroads to invest part of the proceeds of a rate increase in additional box cars. As was noted before, box cars are priced through a collusive "per diem" agreement, not as a result of market processes. Apart from its other undesirable consequences, this system insulates railroad technology from a market test. Given the technology, it is inconceivable that the railroads can provide a quality of service to rival that offered by trucks. Under these circumstances, the nature of changes in demand for freight service simply ensures an indefinite continuation in the decline of the railroads.

---

[20] "The Coupling Connection," *Trains*, April 1975, p. 6.

2
ALTERNATIVE RAILROAD ORGANIZATION AND TECHNOLOGY

The policy implications that follow from the analysis of Chapter 1 are set forth in *Improving Railroad Productivity*. The report argues for the establishment of a competitive transportation industry and, specifically, for an industry organized technologically and geographically so as to be capable of competition. Unfortunately, the present policy framework distorts the incentives of railroad management so greatly that they will not bring forth the changes in technology and in geographical patterns necessary for a competitive railroad industry. Accordingly, the authors of the report proposed reorganizing the industry into a small number (four to seven) of nationwide rail systems. These would presumably be based on the six transcontinental western lines merged with some southern lines, along with trackage purchased from bankrupt and solvent eastern lines.[1]

To implement the report's proposal for a competitive industry, the Interstate Commerce Commission should be abolished and the industry subjected to the ordinary public policy framework of the Sherman Act. There would then be free entry into and free exit out of the transportation industry. The railroads would become integrated transportation companies fulfilling their function in the least costly method, whether by rail, water, or road. Free entry into the industry would ensure an essentially infinite number of truck and barge operators with a high rate of turnover. These operators would be assurances against any exercise of monopoly power by the integrated transportation companies. Any efforts on the part of the integrated companies to price monopolistically would increase the economic range of trucking and make trucking more attractive to

---
[1] *Improving Railroad Productivity*, pp. 321-329.

entrepreneurs. In other words, the integrated transportation companies would have no monopoly power. The industry would be an ordinarily competitive one, unlikely to present any serious problems of public policy, except for the problems of pricing public transportation facilities—roads and waterways.

1. The White Pass & Yukon. As a concomitant of the suggested change in the organization of railroading, the authors of *Improving Railroad Productivity* proposed containerization of general cargo.[2] A container, a semi-trailer body without wheels, is essentially a device for minimizing the costs of intermodal transfer of cargo. This organization of a transportation company is not untried. In particular, the White Pass & Yukon Railway in Alaska and the Yukon Territory of Canada has been organized in this fashion since the mid-1950s.

The rail line of the White Pass & Yukon is a three-foot-gauge railroad between Skagway, Alaska and Whitehorse, Yukon Territory. It has no physical connection with the rest of the Canadian or American railroad system and it has an incompatible gauge. As a consequence, the company chose to integrate itself with the Canadian and American railway system through containerization. It has two containerships which run regularly between Vancouver and Skagway, usually twice a week. Containers are interchanged at Skagway with the railway, which takes them to Whitehorse. They are then taken by truck over the gravel highways of the Yukon Territory to their destination. The Yukon is a large but sparsely populated territory having only about 14,000 people in an area as large as Montana. The cargo inbound to the Yukon is general cargo destined for a wide variety of destinations, mainly mining camps. Outbound, most of the cargo is made up of the products of mines. That cargo also moves in containers to Whitehorse, whence it is taken by rail to Skagway, where some of it is put directly into bulk freighters. The rest moves on the company's containerships to Vancouver, where it is interchanged with American and Canadian railroads, or occasionally with truck lines, and then taken to its destination.[3]

The attractions of this organization for the U.S. railroad system are several. First, the change would allow entrepreneurial decision making to allocate freight between modes, given the existing investment in facilities. The decision about which rail lines to retain and which to abandon would be made in response to market incentives,

---

[2] Ibid., pp. 129-156.
[3] George W. Hilton, "Integration in the North," *Trains*, July 1971, pp. 35-43.

rather than through a process of political resource allocation. This change in the decision-making process would presumably end the political pressure for retaining uneconomic branch lines since, if all general cargo were to arrive in a container, it should be a matter of indifference whether the container arrived by rail or road. In any case, in a competitive market for transportation, no shipper would be receiving a subsidy dependent upon his choice of mode of shipment.

Second, this reorganization of the railroad system is consistent with price competition in transportation. Containers may be handled at a rate based on weight or cubic volume or simply at a flat rate per container by distance, without regard to the contents. In any case, in a competitive market, discriminatory value-of-service rates would be swept away.

Third, and in certain respects most important, the conversion to containerization and the concomitant establishment of intermodal transportation companies would probably bring an end to present railroad technology. This is by no means certain, for the White Pass & Yukon continues to operate with conventional coupling and braking devices. A container car can take about double the optimal switching impact of four miles per hour without damage to the cargo. However, the companies would have an incentive to find the least costly method of moving the containers between points. Because the rail lines of the integrated transportation companies would not interchange equipment, they would not need to use a compatible technology as railroads must at present. Rather, they could experiment individually with alternative technologies.

2. Integral Trains. One such technology has been set forth by engineer John G. Kneiling in his book *Integral Train Systems*.[4] Kneiling proposes containerization of cargo and movement of the cargo by articulated flatbed units about a quarter-mile in length, containing gas turbine engines to power generators which, in turn, would produce electricity for traction motors on axles throughout the articulated units. The cargo would be used for adhesion, as on a rapid transit train. The quarter-mile units could be coupled to one another by a slack-free coupling, with connections for control and braking made electrically. All braking and control impulses would be transmitted instantaneously.

---

[4] John G. Kneiling, *Integral Train Systems* (Milwaukee: Kalmbach Publishing Company, 1969).

With such a technology, trains of infinite length could be run, but increases in the length of the train would not reduce the quality of service or increase the probability of derailment. The technology would be labor-saving, inasmuch as only a single operator would be required at the head of the train, and coupling or uncoupling and brake-line connection could be accomplished by controls on the operator's panel in the cab. The skill level for the entire operation would be relatively low and supervisory personnel would be capable of bringing the railroad through a strike. Classification yards and other present terminal facilities would be replaced by yards serving to transfer containers between rail vehicles and trucks. These would be the analog of container terminals at major ports and would presumably be placed at the outskirts of major cities, so that most trackage in metropolitan areas, as well as most branch lines, could be abandoned.

It is impossible to say whether Kneiling's proposed technology is optimal. Given a reorganized railroad industry, it would be evaluated in the market relative to alternatives, many of which, doubtless, have not even been thought of at present. A conversion of this character could be made entirely with knowledge at hand, applying the ordinary technique of diesel-electric power generation used on present locomotives but stringing out the traction motors under flatbed units of the character Kneiling recommends. Slack-free couplers which make all control and braking connections automatically and which disengage by an electric impulse from the cab have been in use on the New York subway and other electric railways since about 1914. One of the attractions of this proposed conversion would be the ability of the new technology to make use of existing railroad mainlines without much improvement. Articulated units would have relatively low centers of gravity because a high percentage of their weight would be in their trucks. The containers are relatively low with good dynamic properties—low natural frequencies and low wind resistance. Because the cargo would be used for adhesion, trains of this character would be able to round existing curves faster than present equipment and to ascend gradients steeper than those on present mainline railroads. There could be considerable disinvestment in passing tracks and in signaling and local termination facilities, though probably all grade crossings would have to be elevated or depressed—which would represent a significant expense. The White Pass & Yukon has made improvements in and near one tunnel, but otherwise has converted to an intermodal containerized operation without major modifications of the rail line.

In summary, with a conversion of this character, railroads would make more intensive use of existing mainlines, but could divest themselves of the majority of their existing mileage and greatly reduce their present labor forces. Optimal rail mileage for the nation would probably be 40,000 to 70,000 miles.

The discussion up to this point has been concentrated on general cargo moving from a large number of origins to a large number of destinations. The conversion just described is probably not appropriate for bulk cargo. The White Pass & Yukon does containerize its outbound bulk cargo. However, such movements in the United States are increasingly concentrated on single routes—from a given coal mine to a given power station, for example. Unit trains are the most appropriate vehicle for such operations. There is no presumption that they should be run by the companies which own the tracks. There is, in fact, no strong reason why ownership of tracks and operation of trains should be unified in any case. Specialized transportation companies might arrange to use the tracks of railroads for general cargo in a competitive environment; that is the sort of decision, in fact, which we should want to have provided by entrepreneurial decision making in a competitive framework.

The operation of unit trains would be subject to the same rivalry of least-cost technology as the movement of general cargo. Kneiling recommends a hopper-car configuration of integral trains for such movements.[5] Once again alternative devices—many of them not yet in existence—would be brought forth in the rivalry.

3. **The Example of the Merchant Marine.** The conversion to containerized technology recommended here is the analog of the conversion which is taking place rapidly in the world's merchant marines. There it is having a result that one would wish for the railroads. It is undercutting the traditional structure of ocean shipping conferences—which is to say, the cartels of steamship owners. It is lowering the necessary skill level and raising the productivity of maritime labor, and at the same time increasing the degree to which ship operation is automatic. It is also reducing pilferage, labor expense, and accidental damage in longshoring operations.

The maritime conversion is parallel to the proposals set out here for general cargo, though not in general for bulk cargo. Some 90 percent or more of general cargo has proved to be suitable for containerization in ocean shipping operations. The remainder is largely so-called "heavy lift" cargo: locomotives, tanks, equipment for re-

---

[5] Ibid., *passim*.

fineries, and so on. Equipment of this sort might have to be handled on flat-bed units without containerization. The experience of the world's merchant marines, however, indicates the direction in which railroad technology would move in a competitive environment. That, then, should provide the alternative to what is scheduled to take place under the Regional Rail Reorganization Act of 1973.

3
THE REGIONAL RAIL REORGANIZATION ACT OF 1973

Public policy toward the northeastern railroads as embodied in the Regional Rail Reorganization Act of 1973 stemmed from the problems which followed upon the merger of the Pennsylvania Railroad and New York Central Railroad in 1968. The successor Penn Central Transportation Company was unprofitable from the outset. Indeed, it rapidly became the most unprofitable private enterprise in history, losing $82,813,948 in 1969 and four times that amount in 1970. Inability to secure additional financing and to meet an impending loan maturity caused the Penn Central to go bankrupt on Sunday, June 21, 1970. Judge John P. Fullam was appointed in charge of the company on June 23, 1970. On July 22, he appointed as trustees of the company George P. Baker, Richard C. Bond, and Jervis Langdon, Jr.[1]

The framework of policy within which the Penn Central was to be reorganized was Section 77 of the Federal Bankruptcy Act, enacted in 1933. Section 77 had replaced the traditional procedure of selling railroads at receivers' auctions with a process of reorganization in which the financial obligations of a railroad were scaled downward jointly by the courts and the Interstate Commerce Commission. This change in policy was almost universally considered an improvement. Indeed, probably nothing in the entire history of the Interstate Commerce Commission has received such approbation as the commission's implementation of Section 77. The railroads which went bankrupt in the great depression of the 1930s were reorganized conservatively,

---

[1] On the history of the Penn Central bankruptcy generally, see Peter Binzen and Joseph Paughen, *The Wreck of the Penn Central* (New York: Little, Brown & Co., 1971); Michael Gartner, ed., *Riding the Pennsy to Ruin* (New York: Dow, Jones, 1971). A short chronology of events in the bankruptcy proceedings is in *Moody's Transportation Manual*, 1974, pp. 296ff.

with greatly reduced fixed charges, so that the incidence of railroad bankruptcies after World War II was the lowest in American history. The ICC implicitly showed a thoroughly well-grounded and highly appropriate pessimism concerning future railroad earnings.

Section 77 was passed in the depths of the depression and was based on a presumption that the earnings of railroads would recover when the depression had passed. The problems of the Penn Central and the other eastern railroads, however, occurred during a period of prolonged prosperity and there was little or no presumption that changes in business conditions would undo the secular forces operating against them. Accordingly, the policy embodied in Section 77 was of questionable appropriateness to the situation at hand, whatever may have been its past successes. Moreover, although both the Pennsylvania and New York Central dated from the first half of the nineteenth century, neither had ever gone bankrupt before. As a result, the corporate structure of the Penn Central was a model of complexity. Leased lines amounted to 52.8 percent of its 19,459-mile system, and end-of-lease payments by the parent to its subsidiaries made several of them insolvent. Penn Central's management decided to put the principal subsidiaries in bankruptcy in July 1973, in spite of the fact that some of them were not literally insolvent. Two former New York Central subsidiaries, the Peoria & Eastern and the Pittsburgh & Lake Erie, did not join the other major subsidiaries of the Penn Central in bankruptcy.

Judge Fullam directed the trustees to submit a plan for reorganization by September 21, 1971. The trustees filed the plan on April 1, 1972, basing their hopes for solvency on reductions in physical plant and labor costs and on full compensation for the company's passenger losses. In 1972, the Penn Central lost $32.5 million on passenger services provided for Amtrak and $54.7 million on commuter services, virtually all of which were carried on under subsidies by eastern municipal or area-wide transit districts. Jervis Langdon, Jr. was of the opinion that the Penn Central would be an economic property with lines of approximately 11,000 miles, about 57 percent of its current mileage.[2] By January 1, 1973, the trustees had applied to abandon about 3,000 miles of line but received permission to abandon only 800. Similarly, the trustees proposed a new set of work rules cutting freight crews from four to three men, to take effect June 9, 1973. This effort precipitated a strike of twelve hours' duration on

---

[2] *Northeast Rail Transportation*, Hearings before the Subcommittee on Transportation and Aeronautics of the Committee on Interstate and Foreign Commerce, House of Representatives, 93rd Congress, 1st session (1973), p. 248.

February 8, 1973. The trustees concluded the company lacked the strength to suffer a long labor dispute and desisted from the effort to institute the new work rules.

In spite of these reverses, the trustees did have moderate success in reducing the company's losses. In the period from 1970 to 1973, the losses fell from $325,739,148 to $189,002,900, and the company's operating ratio was reduced from 92.08 percent to 82.73 percent. This improvement, such as it was, gave the trustees no reason to believe that the company could be made profitable in the face of union intransigence and ICC insistence on the operation of money-losing branch lines.

Accordingly, on June 29, 1973, the trustees filed with Judge Fullam a plan of reorganization stating that the Penn Central could not be reorganized under Section 77 and proposing a sale of the company's assets, preferably, but not necessarily, for continued rail use. This plan, when filed with the Interstate Commerce Commission on July 5, 1973, caused the ICC to respond that the liquidation plan did not constitute a reorganization plan within the meaning of Section 77 and that liquidation was neither in the public interest nor within the objectives of Section 77.[3]

Meanwhile, much of the rest of the northeastern railroad network had gone into bankruptcy, two companies doing so even before the Penn Central. One, the Central Railroad of New Jersey, had been bankrupt since March 22, 1967. This carrier had abandoned its line to Wilkes-Barre, Pennsylvania, the line which had been its most profitable operation early in the century. What remained was a commuter-carrying and terminal network in northern New Jersey and a line the length of the state which survived by hauling foundry sand. The railroad appeared to have no prospects whatever of profitable operation, and its liquidation had been discussed by its trustees and its court.

The other railroad that preceded the Penn Central into bankruptcy was the Boston & Maine, the dominant railroad of northern New England. This carrier, which went bankrupt on March 12, 1970, could have become profitable by abandoning most of its mileage in New Hampshire. Accordingly, its situation was dissimilar to that of the other eastern bankrupts.

The Penn Central bankruptcy was followed quickly by bankruptcy of the Lehigh Valley on July 24, 1970. The Lehigh Valley was the classic redundant railroad, operating between the port of New York and Buffalo with a relatively long line through difficult terrain

---

[3] *Moody's Transportation Manual*, pp. 296ff.

and country almost devoid of traffic origination. The company's total traffic had sunk to 38 percent of its 1918 peak. Its large-scale traffic origination was limited to an area of about seven miles in and near Bethlehem, Pennsylvania. With no prospect in sight of returning this carrier to profitable operation, its trustees on March 6, 1973 petitioned Judge Fullam, who had been placed in charge of it also, to cease operation on October 1, 1973.[4]

Next, the Reading Company, once the dominant anthracite carrier, filed for bankruptcy on November 23, 1971. This company had existed on anthracite origination and on bridge traffic between the Baltimore & Ohio at Philadelphia and the junction with the Central Railroad of New Jersey at Bound Brook, New Jersey, which is part of the alternate route to the Penn Central's Washington-New York line. This route had come under control of the Chesapeake & Ohio (C&O) when the latter gained control of the Baltimore & Ohio. The C&O apparently considered the Reading and the Central Railroad of New Jersey hopeless and allowed both to go into bankruptcy. The Reading had extensive passenger operations in the suburbs of Philadelphia which were being carried on under local subsidies. The trustees of the Reading were also of the opinion that the company could not be made profitable and proposed to cease operations on November 23, 1973.[5]

The Lehigh & Hudson River, a minor carrier of only eighty-six miles, became bankrupt on April 19, 1972. This railroad had provided a bridge line between the anthracite carriers and the New York, New Haven & Hartford. Partly because of the decline of anthracite and partly because of the new routes for freight following the Penn Central merger, the carrier's traffic had largely disappeared. Its trustees had also concluded by 1973 that the property was hopeless and proposed to cease operation on October 1, 1973.[6]

Next, the Erie Lackawanna Railroad went bankrupt on June 26, 1972.[7] This was a major road of 2,932 miles with a main line from Chicago to New York. This route, though long, was in most respects a good physical property. The railroad was almost devoid of traffic origination outside of Youngstown, Ohio. It served mainly as a long-distance freight carrier and, as such, did moderately well. The deterioration of the Penn Central's physical plant caused many shippers

---

[4] George W. Hilton, "Good News from the Lehigh Valley," *Trains*, August 1973, p. 58.
[5] *Trains*, September 1973, p. 12.
[6] Ibid.
[7] "For EL, the Final Blow," *Trains*, September 1972, pp. 6, 8.

to prefer the Erie Lackawanna. It was controlled by Dereco, a subsidiary of the Norfolk & Western. Together with the Delaware & Hudson, which was not bankrupt, and the Boston & Maine, it provided an alternative route to the Penn Central's between Chicago and Boston. The Erie Lackawanna's mileage in northern Pennsylvania and southern New York State was severely harmed by hurricane Agnes in the early summer of 1972, causing the company to become insolvent unexpectedly and to file for bankruptcy. The trustees of this company, like their counterparts on the Boston & Maine, believed the railroad could be restored to profitability and until late in 1974 presumed that the company could be reorganized under Section 77.

Finally, the Ann Arbor Railroad went bankrupt on November 1, 1973. This carrier, with a line from Toledo, Ohio to Frankfort, Michigan, was built to be integral with a railroad car ferry operation on four routes across Lake Michigan. The ferry operation had become thoroughly uneconomic because of high labor expenses; two of its four routes had been abandoned, and the company was endeavoring to get rid of the remaining two together with the northernmost portion of the rail line. The southern portion could probably have been reorganized into a weak short line serving minor plants of the automobile industry.[8]

The eight bankrupt railroads totaled 26,790 miles, 72.6 percent of them belonging to the Penn Central. These lines comprised somewhat more than 50 percent of the rail mileage in the northeastern United States. Most of the rest was divided between two systems, both of which remain moderately profitable. One is the Chesapeake & Ohio which had come to control the Baltimore & Ohio. Although these carriers had not been merged, they operate essentially as one railroad. The other is the Norfolk & Western (N&W), which had merged with or leased the Nickel Plate Road and the Wabash. Both these systems subsidize their unprofitable mileage in the Northeast with coal traffic on the C&O and N&W main lines, and neither is threatened with insolvency. In addition, there were solvent independents in the Northeast: the Detroit, Toledo & Ironton, the Delaware & Hudson, the Bessemer & Lake Erie, the Maine Central, the Bangor & Aroostook, and some short lines.

This, to sum up, was the situation which confronted Congress in late 1973: The largest railroad in the country by volume of freight traffic, the Penn Central, was threatened with cessation of service. Several lesser bankrupt lines might also cease operation. Two bank-

---

[8] George W. Hilton, "Great Lakes Car Ferries: An Endangered Species," *Trains*, January 1975, pp. 42-51.

rupt railroads had at least some prospects of returning to profitable operation, and two large solvent systems which competed with the Penn Central had every prospect of profitable operation for the near future.

The Nixon administration preferred a solution which would leave the bankrupt railroads under private ownership and which would place the financing of their reorganization, as far as possible, outside of the federal budget. The railroad industry was also eager to avoid nationalization of the bankrupts. Precedents for economic organization with nominal private ownership but under public control lay in the Federal National Mortgage Association, COMSAT and especially in the National Railroad Passenger Corporation, commonly known as Amtrak. The last of these provided a prototype for a joint, private-federal corporation to operate the insolvent northeastern railroads. Amtrak had succeeded to the passenger operations of the American railroads (with four exceptions) in 1971 and was being operated under ownership of the member railroads but under federal control with extensive federal subsidy.

The content of the Regional Rail Reorganization Act of 1973 was worked out mainly by the president of the Union Pacific Railroad, Frank Barnett, and his general counsel, William J. MacDonald, in collaboration with Jervis Langdon, Jr.[9] The labor provisions were developed by Al Chesser, president of the United Transportation Union, and C. L. Dennis, chief of the Brotherhood of Airline and Railroad Clerks, in collaboration with the presidents of some major railroads. The bill was supported by the Association of American Railroads and sponsored in Congress by Representatives Brock Adams (D-Wash.) and Richard Shoup (R-Mont.), both members of the Transportation and Aeronautics Subcommittee of the House of Representatives. The bill was brought through to passage in December 1973 as the Regional Rail Reorganization Act of 1973, although President Nixon did not sign it into law until January 2, 1974.

Content of the Act

The act provided a tripartite organization to undertake the task of restructuring the northeastern railroads.[10] This organization consists of the following: (1) the U.S. Railway Association, established within the Department of Transportation for the purpose of planning and

---

[9] A detailed history of the development of the act is in Joseph Albright, "The Penn Central: A Hell of a Way to Run a Government," *The New York Times Magazine*, November 3, 1974, pp. 16ff.
[10] Public Law 93-236.

organizing the Consolidated Rail Corporation; (2) ConRail itself, which is to be the operating entity, analogous to Amtrak, of the new railroad; and (3) the Rail Services Planning Office, established within the Interstate Commerce Commission for the purpose of holding hearings on and evaluating the U.S. Railway Association's proposals. It was expected that these three bodies would bring forth a consolidated northeastern railroad of about 15,000 to 19,000 miles.

An elaborate sequence of reporting and decision making is provided for in the act. Within thirty days of passage, the secretary of transportation was required to submit to Congress recommendations for the organization of the system. Within 120 days, the judges in bankruptcy had to decide between reorganization under Section 77 or transfer of the railroads which they supervise to the United States Railway Association for inclusion in the Consolidated Rail Corporation. The corporation, usually known as ConRail, is to be privately owned and is intended to be a profit-making enterprise. The U.S. Railway Association is to be governed by a board consisting of representatives of the federal government, the Association of American Railroads, the AFL-CIO, the National Governors Conference, the National League of Cities, and the Conference of Mayors, along with representatives of shippers' organizations and financial interests.

The United States Railway Association is empowered to issue obligations up to $1.5 billion, of which $1 billion may go to ConRail. Of that $1 billion, at least $500 million must be spent for rehabilitation and modernization of ConRail properties. The additional $500 million is earmarked for improvements on the Washington-New York-Boston passenger line, which is expected to be sold or leased to Amtrak. The U.S. Railway Association may make loans to ConRail and Amtrak and to other railroads which connect with the bankrupts, are themselves bankrupt, or are engaged in an effort to avoid bankruptcy. This provision was written into the law to allow financial aid to two extremely weak midwestern and southwestern carriers, the Chicago, Rock Island & Pacific and the Missouri-Kansas-Texas, neither of which was then bankrupt. Subsequently, the Rock Island went bankrupt on March 17, 1975.[11] The act provided $85 million in interim aid to bankrupt railroads to allow them to keep operating during the transitional period.

By the act, the U.S. Railway Association was directed to survey the northeastern United States from Maine to Illinois for traffic density and patterns and to publish its results as source material for a Preliminary System Plan for future rail service, taking into con-

---

[11] "A Tide in CRI&P Affairs," *Trains*, June 1975, pp. 3-4, 6.

sideration impact on solvent carriers, future passenger service, effect on employees, joint use of facilities, and other relevant factors. The Rail Services Planning Office was directed to evaluate the results of this survey and to respond within ninety days. Within 180 days it was to publish standards for determining revenue, avoidable costs, and reasonable returns.

The act provides $90 million in federal funds for each of the next two fiscal years for subsidy of branch lines on a 70/30 basis, $70 in federal funds matching each $30 in local funds—the ratio long used for contributions to the federal aid highway network. Such funds are to be available if the subsidy is less than the cost to society of abandonment, including the cost of transportation by rival modes, the loss of output, the cost of relocation or welfare benefits to displaced personnel, pollution, added fuel costs, and other relevant considerations.

According to the schedule set forth in the act, the U.S. Railway Association was to publish its Preliminary System Plan within 300 days of the law's enactment. The Rail Services Planning Office was to report, after holding hearings, 60 days later. The U.S. Railway Association was then to submit a final plan to its board within 60 days, and the board was to vote on it and submit it to Congress within 30 days. The ICC was to report to Congress in another 30 days. The final plan was to be approved if neither house of Congress passed a resolution of disapproval within 60 days after receiving the plan. On this time schedule, the final plan would have been accepted or rejected by Congress by May 26, 1975 and submitted to the bankruptcy courts on August 24, 1975. The Consolidated Rail Corporation would have begun operation 20 days later. However, given the magnitude of the planning procedure, it was impossible to keep the schedule. The U.S. Railway Association's final plan was submitted to Congress on July 26, 1975.

Under the terms of the act, ConRail is to be established by an exchange of railroad properties for ConRail stock: a similar transfer of rolling stock in exchange for equity was made in the establishment of Amtrak. Properties not included in ConRail may be sold to solvent railroads or to Amtrak or to state highway departments. ConRail is to have the legal status of a profit-seeking common carrier railroad. It is prohibited from engaging in nonrailroad activities until it has paid off half its indebtedness to the federal government. Employee stock ownership in the corporation is explicitly encouraged.

The act provides generous income protection for employees—including, for example, displacement allowances of up to $2,500 a month until age sixty-five for employees with five years of service as of January 2, 1974 and lump-sum separation allowances of up to $20,000 for employees terminated by ConRail. Aggregate appropriations of $250 million are authorized for such purposes.

Formative Procedures under the Act

At present (July 1975), the formative procedures of the ConRail system have advanced through the issuance of the U.S. Railway Association's Preliminary System Plan on February 26, 1975,[12] the evaluation of that plan by the Rail Services Planning Office of the Interstate Commerce Commission,[13] and the submission to Congress of the proposed Final System Plan of the U.S. Railway Association on July 26, 1975.[14]

In its Preliminary System Plan, the U.S. Railway Association rejected the alternatives of (1) controlled liquidation of the Penn Central, and (2) creation of two rival federal systems, one based on the former Pennsylvania and the other based on the former New York Central, or (3) creation of a unified ConRail system including properties of all the northeastern bankrupts. Instead, the association recommended a single ConRail system consisting of the Penn Central, the Reading (minus the lines required to give the C&O connections with the Delaware & Hudson and the Lehigh Valley for connections to New England and New York, respectively), the Lehigh Valley between Newark, New Jersey, and Waverly, New York, the Central Railroad of New Jersey, the Pennsylvania-Reading Seashore Lines, the Lehigh & Hudson River, and the Ann Arbor. It also recommended that the East Coast line of the Penn Central be turned over to Amtrak and that about 6,200 miles of branch lines be abandoned or turned over to other operators in the federal subsidy arrangement established in the act. Under this plan, the ConRail system would amount to about 15,000 miles of railroad.

---

[12] "Preliminary System Plan for Restructuring Railroads in the Northeast and Midwest Region Pursuant to the Regional Rail Reorganization Act of 1973," February 26, 1975, 3 vols. (Washington, D.C.: U.S. Government Printing Office, 1975).

[13] "Evaluation of the U.S. Railway Association's Preliminary System Plan," Report of the Rail Services Planning Office to the U.S. Railway Association (Washington, D.C.: Interstate Commerce Commission, April 28, 1975).

[14] United States Railway Association, "Final System Plan for Restructuring Railroads in the Northeast and Midwest Region Pursuant to the Regional Rail Reorganization Act of 1973," July 26, 1975, 2 vols. (Washington, D. C.: U.S. Government Printing Office, 1975).

The Preliminary System Plan dealt only in tentative fashion with the Erie Lackawanna, whose trustees recently (January 9, 1975) reversed their position and decided on inclusion of their system in ConRail rather than reorganization under Section 77. The U.S. Railway Association's proposal was (1) that the Norfolk & Western take the Erie Lackawanna's lines between Buffalo and Newark, thereby restoring the traditional Nickel Plate-Lackawanna line between Chicago and New York via Buffalo, and (2) that the former Erie lines to Chicago and Dayton, west of Marion, Ohio, were to be abandoned.

The preliminary plan also proposed that the Chesapeake & Ohio system be extended from Philadelphia to Allentown over the Reading and that the Delaware & Hudson be given trackage rights over the Lehigh Valley from Wilkes-Barre to Allentown to connect with the C&O system. These arrangements would ensure the Delaware & Hudson connections with the Norfolk & Western system at Binghamton and with the Chesapeake & Ohio system at Allentown. The Delaware & Hudson's principal traffic to the interchange with the Boston & Maine at Mechanicville, New York, would then be secured. As an alternative in the event of noncooperation by the Norfolk & Western and Chesapeake & Ohio, the report proposed establishment of a Middle Atlantic Railroad Corporation based on the Erie Lackawanna together with portions of the Central Railroad of New Jersey, the Lehigh Valley, and the Reading to provide an east-west line rival to the ConRail system.

The U.S. Railway Association proposed a fourteen-year program of rehabilitation of track and facilities at the cost of $5 billion, and a ten-year, $2.3 billion program for the purchase and rehabilitation of freight cars. It also proposed restoration or expansion of passenger service between eighteen city pairs, including New York-Boston and New York-Washington, mainly on routes of intermediate distance, such as Cincinnati-Detroit, Cincinnati-Cleveland, Pittsburgh-Cleveland, Buffalo-Cleveland, Chicago-Cleveland, and Washington-Norfolk.

In addition to the plans which the U.S. Railway Association has made under the act of 1973, it proposed the establishment of an additional federal authority, the Consolidated Facilities Corporation, or ConFac, which would use funds provided by the government, or funds from loans guaranteed by the government, to buy and rehabilitate railroad rights-of-way and structures. This proposal embodies a frequent suggestion that the federal government own the facilities and rent them to users as in the fashion of airports and highways.

By coincidence, simultaneously with the release of the U.S. Railway Association's preliminary report, Congress approved $347 million in emergency aid to keep the Penn Central and the other bankrupts operating.[15]

In its preliminary report, the U.S. Railway Association anticipated that its proposal would allow the bankrupt railroads to return to profitable operation within a three-year period. The report's projections showed losses before taxes of $91 million in 1976 and $27 million in 1977, but profits thereafter of $32 million in 1978 growing to $382 million in 1985 (all in 1973 dollars). Subsequently these projections were revised (see pages 42–43).

John T. Fishwick, president of the Norfolk & Western Railway, has been particularly critical of the suggestions contained in the preliminary plan.[16] He estimates that federal expenditure on the ConRail system would be about double what the report projected. The projections presume a reversal of the secular decline in the traffic of the northeastern railroads and, in particular, a reversal of the severe decline in their coal traffic. Fishwick has also pointed out that the projections envisage a reduction of ConRail's operating ratio to 74 percent by 1985. This ratio is comparable to those of the strongest railroads—that is, the Norfolk & Western, the Chesapeake & Ohio, the Southern, and the Union Pacific in 1973. Indeed, the ratio is more favorable than that of any American railroad but the Southern. The Penn Central was in fact moving in the opposite direction. Its operating ratio rose from 79.27 percent in November 1973 to 86.17 percent by November 1974. The system's net loss had increased from $11.4 million for November 1973 to $26.6 million for November 1974, and management anticipated a loss of approximately a million dollars per day in the first quarter of 1975.[17]

Pessimism concerning ConRail's prospects is fairly universal. Gellman Research Associates, in an evaluation of the Preliminary System Plan for the Rail Services Planning Office, demonstrated how dependent were the projected earnings of ConRail on the U.S. Railway Association's estimates of operating costs, rehabilitation cost, interest rates, and projected traffic. If the association's projections of

---

[15] "Rail Rescue Funds Cleared by Senate," *New York Times*, February 27, 1975, p. 1.

[16] Statement of John T. Fishwick on behalf of the Norfolk & Western Railway Company, in "Review of the United States Railway Association's Preliminary System Plan: Rail Services Planning Office Hearings," March 27, 1975 (Washington, D.C.: ICC, Rail Services Planning Office, 1975).

[17] "$1,000,000 a Day—In Cash," *Trains*, March 1975, pp. 4, 8.

costs and total revenue were overly optimistic by three-quarters of 1 percent, ConRail would have a cumulative net deficit of $368 million from 1976 through 1985, rather than a cumulative net income of $1,699 million.[18]

It is probably impossible at present to estimate with accuracy the prospective losses of the ConRail system when formed. Professor Paul W. MacAvoy, a member of the Council of Economic Advisers, has estimated the prospective annual federal subsidy of ConRail as being in the range from $500 million to $1.5 billion.[19]

Inevitably, a considerable number of alternatives to the plan have been formulated. John T. Fishwick has proposed nationalization of the lines east of Albany and Harrisburg, lines which were hopelessly unprofitable, and either ordinary reorganization under Section 77 of the western lines of the Penn Central system or transfer of some portions of that mileage to other carriers with selective abandonment of the lines.[20] Academic opinion strongly favors transfer of Penn Central properties to solvent carriers. Ten academic economists met with Secretary of Transportation William T. Coleman, Jr. on April 11, 1975, and recommended rejection of the Preliminary System Plan in favor of some form of transfer of the bankrupt properties to solvent carriers outside the Northeast. The present organization of the Penn Central into numerous subsidiaries would facilitate such a transfer: the subsidiaries can be auctioned off individually and, within the constraints of the present organization of the industry, would go to their highest valued use. These economists stated that the ConRail proposal amounted to de facto nationalization of rail services in the northeast because ConRail could not be self-sufficient in the long run.[21]

A different—indeed, essentially opposite—set of observations and policies was contained in the report of the ICC's Rail Services

---

[18] Gellman Research Associates, Inc., "Summary of Seminar on Financial Analysis of the Preliminary System Plan Presented to the Office of the Public Counsel [of the Rail Services Planning Office]," February 27, 1975, Exhibit 5 (Jenkintown, Pa., 1975).

[19] *Washington Post*, June 13, 1975, p. D12.

[20] Fishwick, "Review of the United States Railway Association's Preliminary System Plan."

[21] "Academic Community Views on the Preliminary System Plan," memorandum to Secretary of Transportation William T. Coleman, Jr., representing a consensus of the views of W. Bruce Allen, Allen R. Ferguson, Aaron J. Gellman, George W. Hilton, Alan MacAdams, Alexander L. Morton, James C. Nelson, Robert A. Nelson, William F. Hamilton, and James C. Miller III. The members of this panel differed on methods of implementing the transfer, but were unanimous in their overall recommendation.

Planning Office of April 28, 1975. The ICC is directed by the act to gather information concerning the proposed plan in a fashion analogous to its procedures in connection with branch line abandonment. It held hearings around the country on the branch lines that had been treated as possibly expendable in the U.S. Railway Association's first report on the northeastern railroads. The commission, it should be remembered, has been engaging in cross-subsidy arrangements typical of regulatory commissions, subsidizing branch-line operations out of main-line earnings. This has paralleled its cross-subsidy of passenger service out of freight earnings. Main-line service in the Northeast has not been profitable enough to allow this cross-subsidy for some time, just as freight service ceased to be profitable enough to cross-subsidize passenger service a decade and more earlier. The commission followed parallel courses in these situations, seeking, in both, outright federal funds to substitute for the cross-subsidy. Thus, the Rail Services Planning Office report proposed a $12 billion effort to rehabilitate the nation's railroads, to be financed by taxes on the fuel used by railroads, trucks (but not buses), and inland river towboats, and also on electric power output. This report recommended a two-year moratorium on branch-line abandonment while more accurate data were being gathered on the situation.[22]

The ICC report was in accord with the political pressures that were being widely voiced in the eastern states. In the U.S. Railway Association's preliminary report, Pennsylvania was to retain 41 percent of its mileage and lose another 41 percent through abandonment, while decision was postponed on the remaining 18 percent. Governor Milton J. Shapp, a longstanding opponent of the Penn Central merger, considered the proposed reduction of mileage in his state a threat to the state's economy. He proposed a rail trust fund of about $13 billion to be raised over a six-year period from a 5 percent surcharge on all railroad freight.[23] This, too, would have been a form of cross-subsidy, for the tax would have been paid very largely by shippers in other parts of the country.

Other observers have supported the earlier proposals for dividing the Penn Central between the former New York Central and the Pennsylvania lines and for establishing the Middle Atlantic Rail Corporation. At present, however, it appears that a form of the single ConRail system proposal will be implemented. On May 29,

---

[22] "Evaluation of the U.S. Railway Association's Preliminary System Plan," summary on pp. 3-8.
[23] "Can Low Volume Rail Lines Still Be Justified?" *New York Times*, June 2, 1975, p. 42.

1975, the directors of the U.S. Railway Association voted seven to one to proceed with the single ConRail plan,[24] and on July 26 that proposal was submitted to the Congress.

The Final System Plan presented to Congress on July 26, 1975 entailed the following:

—Establishment of a single ConRail system of about 15,000 miles. The mileage proposed for abandonment is reduced from 6,200 to 5,700. The lines projected for abandonment handle only about 2 percent of the traffic in the region.

—Sale to the Chesapeake & Ohio for $104 million of most of the Reading's main lines plus the east end of the Erie Lackawanna from a junction with the Baltimore & Ohio at Sterling, Ohio, to Buffalo and the New York terminal area of New Jersey. The west end of the Erie Lackawanna will be replaced by the Baltimore & Ohio main line. The C&O will also receive entry into Charleston, West Virginia. This change from the preliminary plan reflects the N&W's unwillingness to accept the Erie Lackawanna's eastern lines.

—Transfer to ConRail from the C&O system of the B&O-Reading-Central Railroad of New Jersey-Washington-New York line.

—Transfer to the Norfolk & Western of the Penn Central's track from Cincinnati to New Castle, Indiana, to shorten the N&W's mileage from Norfolk to Kansas City. The N&W is also to receive trackage rights on ConRail from Hagerstown to Harrisburg to achieve a connection with the Delaware & Hudson, which is to buy the Penn Central track from Wilkes-Barre to Sunbury and take trackage rights on ConRail from Sunbury to Harrisburg.

—Transfer of the Penn Central's line on the Delmarva Peninsula, including the Norfolk-Cape Charles ferry, to the Southern Railway.

—Transfer to the Grand Trunk Western of Penn Central terminal lines in Saginaw, Midland and Bay City, Michigan. In a similar effort to strengthen the independent railroads in the area, trackage rights are to be granted the Detroit-Toledo & Ironton to reach Cincinnati, the Pittsburgh & Lake Erie to reach Ashtabula, and the Toledo-Peoria & Western to achieve some connection with ConRail in north-central Indiana.

—Transfer to Amtrak of the Washington-Boston passenger line.

---

[24] "NE Rail Competition Pledged," *Washington Post*, June 11, 1975, pp. D1-2.

It is also proposed that Amtrak acquire the former Michigan Central main line from Porter, Indiana, to Kalamazoo, Michigan, for its Chicago-Detroit passenger service.

ConRail is to issue to the U.S. Railway Association $1 billion in debentures and $850 million in Series A preferred stock, both at 7.5 percent interest. The federal government is to have priority among creditors in the event of default on securities. Total investment in ConRail's projected capital program over the first ten years is estimated at $6,029 million, of which $1,841 million is to come from the proceeds of the securities issued to the U.S. Railway Association, $1,252 million from the private sector (for equipment financing), and $2,936 from retained earnings. The acquisition cost of the system is uncertain, but the U.S. Railway Association estimates the net liquidation value of the bankrupts at $621 million. Because the Penn Central estimates its scrap value at $2 billion, an effort to acquire the bankrupts at a price as low as the Association's figure would presumably entail adjudication. ConRail's earnings are projected at a loss of $332 million in 1976, followed by several years of reduced unprofitability, and then profits of $36 million in 1979 and growing to $597 million in 1985.[25]

It should be noted that the projections in the final plan differ from those in the preliminary plan in that profits are expected to come one year later but to be greater in magnitude. Also the plan leaves the ultimate question of continued operation of ConRail versus controlled transfer of properties to solvent railroads up to Congress.

The Ford administration announced its support for the Final System, but suggested that implementation be accompanied by enactment of the administration's current proposal for partial rate deregulation.

---

[25] United States Railway Association, "Final System Plan," p. 51.

4
EVALUATION

It should be apparent from a comparison of Chapters 2 and 3 that the Regional Rail Reorganization Act of 1973 represents the antithesis of the policies which should be followed according to the analysis set forth in *Improving Railroad Productivity*.[1] The principal implications of that report were that the regional pattern of railroads should be ended, that the present technology of the Janney coupler and the Westinghouse air brake should be replaced through a competitive effort of railroads to find one or more alternatives, and that the present economic organization in which the railroads are simultaneously rivals and joint venturers should be replaced with one in which they are competitive firms operating under the antitrust policy embodied in the Sherman Act. The act of 1973 moves public policy in an opposing course in each case.

Consequences of the Act

First, the Regional Rail Reorganization Act preserves the balkanized regional railroad pattern. It perpetuates the merger of the Penn Central, which stemmed from the inappropriate incentives given railroad management by the present organization of the industry. If the proposed ConRail system takes shape, it will consist of the merged Penn Central, less some of its branch lines and redundant main lines, plus additional trackage from the other bankrupts, apparently resulting in a railroad slightly smaller than the existing Penn Central. The transfer of properties to the C&O will be done

---

[1] The antithetical character of the policies has been noted by the *Wall Street Journal* in "A Rational Rail Plan," May 13, 1975, p. 22.

by administrative decision making so as to preserve traditional routings, rather than by market processes which would direct trackage to its highest valued use. Also, the properties will be transferred to a northeastern system rather than to a solvent carrier from another area.

The 1973 act explicitly prevents the industry from moving in the direction of nationwide rail systems. If the Final System Plan is implemented, there can be no further transfer of bankrupt lines to solvent carriers without further congressional enactment. In their liquidation plan of 1973, the trustees of the Penn Central proposed to sell off the railroad in pieces and, as noted above, the Penn Central's present organization of leased subsidiaries would facilitate this. Several creditors had earlier proposed a similar liquidation to Judge Fullam. Recently, the Milwaukee Road, the weakest of the western transcontinental railroads, indicated its interest in acquiring the lease of the Penn Central's Panhandle lines, which are the former Pennsylvania's secondary main line from Pittsburgh to Chicago and St. Louis via Columbus and Indianapolis.[2] Given its present physical condition and to some extent its geographical pattern, this is the least attractive of the leased subsidiaries and thus probably the one which would enable the Milwaukee Road to extend itself to Pittsburgh in the least costly fashion. Competitive pressures on other western railroads would be likely to cause them to bid for other portions of the Penn Central system in the absence of the policy currently being implemented.

Similarly, the Southern Railway indicated its interest in acquiring the Penn Central's Delmarva Peninsula line, including the Cape Charles-Norfolk car ferry, so as to gain an interchange with the Baltimore & Ohio and Reading at Wilmington, Delaware.[3] Two recent studies by consulting firms demonstrate the financial ability of the eight major solvent railroads to acquire the Penn Central's lines west of Albany and Harrisburg.[4]

---

[2] Testimony of Worthington L. Smith, president of Chicago, Milwaukee, St. Paul & Pacific Railroad Company, in the matter of Northeastern Railroad Investigation: "Comments on Preliminary System Plan of United States Railway Association," Ex Parte No. 293 (Sub. 5), 1975 (Washington, D. C.: ICC, Rail Services Planning Office, 1975).

[3] Letter of W. Graham Claytor, Jr., president of the Southern Railway, to Paul F. Cruikshank, vice-president of the U.S. Railway Association, January 8, 1975.

[4] Gellman Research Associates, Inc., "Final Report: Feasibility Analysis of Controlled Transfer for the United States Department of Transportation," 3 vols., May 9, 1975 (Jenkintown, Pa.); Economics and Science Planning, "Feasibility of a Controlled Transfer of Bankrupt Rail Lines to Solvent Railroads," April 17, 1975 (Washington, D. C.).

Second, the present incentive structure for the managements of the bankrupt eastern railroads is replaced not with the incentives motivating a competitive firm, but rather with a mixture of present incentives and a large number of pressures for political resource allocation.

It was noted in Chapter 3 that the U.S. Railway Association, which is setting up the ConRail system, is governed by a board representing the federal government, the Association of American Railroads, the AFL-CIO, the National Governors Council, the National League of Cities, and the Conference of Mayors, along with representatives of shippers and the financial community. Representatives of shippers, unions, state governments and local governments will have incentives to preserve branch lines either under cross-subsidy or explicit subsidy. The new organization planned for the northeastern railroads represents a shift from cross-subsidies to explicit subsidies, just as the Amtrak system did.

Now, with approximately four years of experience under Amtrak to enable us to judge the effect of such an organization, we find that Amtrak has not been able to provide a geographical pattern of rail service which, given the constraints governing the system, would have been optimal. Rather, it has been under strong political pressures to provide rail service in uneconomic areas on the basis of the fortuitous geographical pattern of the political strength of the men and women who are concerned with formulating or funding American transportation policy. West Virginia and Montana, which were represented in Congress or on the Interstate Commerce Commission by figures who were powerful politically, received relatively dense networks of rail passenger services, whereas at the beginning of the Amtrak program, cities as large as Cleveland and Dallas were not included. The change in incentives from those influencing Penn Central's management to those that would guide the management of ConRail should be expected to make ConRail more costly to operate than the Penn Central rather than less costly, as the Preliminary System Plan of the U.S. Railway Association projects.

Third, the Regional Rail Reorganization Act of 1973 directly preserves present technology. The act will put between $1 billion and $1.5 billion into rights-of-way. Northeastern rights-of-way, given present technology, must be considerably upgraded if trains are to operate through the fifteen-to-thirty-miles-per-hour range at which track-train dynamic interactions are greatest. The U.S. Railway Association's Preliminary System Plan proposes investing as much as $7 billion in rehabilitation, including $700 million in locomotives and in the purchase or major repair of 20,000 freight cars. This would perpetuate the present technology of separate locomotives and separate freight cars with Janney couplers and the Westinghouse air brake. These cars are expected to continue to circulate about the railroad system in interchange as they now do, with the same problems of damage on impact and uncertainty of arrival. Thus, the investment will serve only to restore a technology which will continue to fail a market test in competition with trucking.

Fourth, the act preserves the present economic organization of the railroad industry. The ConRail system is to be a common carrier operating within the same framework of public policy as do existing railroads. Nothing in the act promises liberalization of present union operating rules. Indeed, the act should strengthen unions in several respects. The protection of displaced employees with five-year service by providing them with incomes of up to $2,500 per month or lump-sum separation allowances of up to $20,000 amounts to protection of job rights in excess of present protection. In addition, the new capital to be brought into the industry will be of the kind that is complementary to labor rather than a substitution for labor—that is, capital in the form of traditional locomotives, freight cars, and improvements to rights-of-way. By application of Alfred Marshall's joint demand analysis, making the industry more capital-intensive in this way will reduce the elasticity of demand for labor and thus strengthen the unions. The changes in technology proposed in Chapter 2, in contrast, would substitute capital for labor, lower the skill level, and reduce the strength of the unions.

Analogies to Other Programs

The act of 1973 represents an extreme example of denying a market test. Even those who are not generally committed to accepting market tests might be expected to conclude that an enterprise losing approximately $1 million a day is inappropriately organized. The denial of a market test in this instance, though extraordinary in magnitude, is not exceptional for government programs. Apart from Amtrak, to which analogies have been drawn frequently in this study, several federal programs have the same general character of denying a market test and accepting an inappropriate economic organization, frequently one that is combined with improper pricing of public facilities. The expenditure of government funds then treats the symptoms—not the causes—of the inappropriate organization and typically aggravates the problem.

The Federal Airport Aid Program represents this kind of treatment of symptoms. The airlines are a cartelized industry operating under the Civil Aeronautics Board. Cartelization gives them an incentive to fly too frequently with load factors that are too low. Airports are in the public sector, run by airport authorities that do not seek to maximize net receipts but rather endeavor simply to break even. These authorities price the runways which they are allocating on a simple average-total-cost pricing system, charging a fee levied usually on the basis of the weight of the aircraft without regard to the hour at which the runway is used. The combination of the incentives in the cartel with the pricing policies of the airport authorities generates an excess demand for runways in peak hours. The federal government responds with the Federal Airport Aid Program. This program proliferates airports in cities which have too little traffic to support them, creates redundant airports in major cities, and fails to solve the problem of excess demand in peak periods at existing large-city airports.[5]

The Urban Mass Transportation Assistance programs represent a similar response to the inappropriate organization of urban transit systems and to a pricing of roads analogous to the pricing of airport runways. Urban transit is provided by a series of city-wide or area-wide monopolies, although bus technology would permit competitive organization. The transit authorities, despite the conversion to buses, perpetuate the old economic organization of the street railways—a large vehicle which stops frequently, fixed routes involving mainly a radial pattern from the central business district, and unionized employees. These enterprises provide a service of about the quality of streetcars and, as a consequence, have declined steadily relative to the automobile.

To the inappropriate organization of transit has been added the practice of pricing streets and roads of all sorts by an excise on gasoline undifferentiated by the place and hour in which the driving takes place, which in turn produces consequences like those of the pricing of airport runways. The Urban Mass Transportation Assistance Program has been mainly a series of capital grants, which have made more capital-intensive an industry which was already, by its organization, excessively capital-intensive. It has tended to strengthen the union in the industry, increase the incentives to travel at peak

---

[5] Ross D. Eckert, *Airports and Congestion* (Washington, D. C.: American Enterprise Institute for Public Policy Research, 1972).

hours and to make long home-work trips, and in other respects worsen the problem with which it was intended to deal.[6]

In both the airport and urban transit programs, the problem has been a combination of an inappropriate economic organization and an undesirable method of pricing of public facilities. Superficially the ConRail program appears to incorporate only the first of these, an undesirable organization of an industry. The Preliminary System Plan of the U.S. Railway Association, however, recommended nationalization of rights-of-way into the ConFac system, a proposal which, if implemented, would make the policy of the ConRail system on all grounds parallel to airport and transit policy. There is no way of knowing how ConFac would price the services of rights-of-way. But, because it would be a public body whose directors would be in no position to capture any entrepreneurial gain from appropriate pricing of facilities, there is every reason to expect it to use average-cost pricing devices of the sort used by airport authorities and highway administrators.

Policies of the character under discussion are not limited to transportation. The hospital industry, for example, is made up mainly of eleemosynary institutions, which is to say, firms that do not maximize net receipts. In addition, because a third party intervenes between the demanders and suppliers of the service, namely the Blue Cross system or one of its counterparts, the normal incentive to economize on the provision of the supply is not provided. The Hill-Burton Act of 1947 deals with the excess demand created in this fashion by providing for grants to build hospitals or additions to existing hospitals. The policy causes a reduction in the occupancy rate for hospitals and a decline in the share of the industry occupied by proprietary hospitals—that is, hospitals which do seek to maximize net receipts. As in the previous examples, the policy tends to perpetuate and aggravate the problem with which it is designed to deal.[7]

Finally, the college dormitory program of the federal government is similar in its origins and in its consequences. Colleges and universities are also non-profit-maximizing institutions. They maximize prestige instead of money, and tend to build impressive physical plants—frequently in remote areas—from which no one in authority can capture any entrepreneurial gains by full use. More than half

---

[6] George W. Hilton, *Federal Transit Subsidies* (Washington, D. C.: American Enterprise Institute for Public Policy Research, 1974).

[7] Judith R. Lave and Lester B. Lave, *The Hospital Construction Act* (Washington, D. C.: American Enterprise Institute for Public Policy Research, 1974).

the industry is in the public sector, mainly run by state governments. State institutions charge on the average about 17 percent of average total costs. The private institutions, being confronted by rivals which are virtually giving away their products, charge fees amounting to only about 50 percent of average total cost. They endeavor to finance the remainder from income from endowment, grants from public bodies, and contributions from alumni whose loyalty they endeavor to engender through the generation of prestige. Like most nonprofit institutions they tend to underprice their output, thereby generating an excess demand so that the administrators may capture benefits in the form of gratitude. Such considerations lead private institutions to favor children of alumni for admission.

The fact that universities are not maximizing net receipts causes their faculty members to place an exceptional value on freedom from the prospect of arbitrary discharge. This causes a demand for security of employment (except in cases of dereliction of duty or malfeasance) which is, of course, known as academic tenure. The universities, whose administrators have nothing to lose in a pecuniary sense through mistakes in granting of tenure, are more than ordinarily willing to accede to such demands.

The net effect of this organization of higher education is to prevent universities from expanding and contracting normally in response to increases and decreases in demand. Both increases and decreases tend to be looked upon as disastrous. When an increase in demand occurs, as in the 1960s, administrators conclude that additional students will be educated at a loss. When a decrease in demand occurs, as in the 1970s, the administrators conclude that their institutions cannot afford the loss of revenue. Thus university administrators almost invariably conclude that their institutions are currently at optimal size. Academic tenure prevents them from reducing their labor force in normal fashion when diminutions in demand occur. The college dormitory program creates a parallel situation in the physical plant. The federal government assists in constructing dormitories to deal with increases in demand, but since the universities are to some extent outside the market nexus, there is no mechanism by which their physical plant will go to its highest valued use. When the country is experiencing an increase in the number of the aged and a diminution in a number of college-age youth, the economic organization of higher education does not in general allow the dormitories to be reallocated for the purpose of housing the aged. Accordingly, the dormitory program creates sunk investments which are analogous to the faculty with tenure, thereby aggravating what is already wrong with American higher education.[8]

These four examples do not exhaust the catalog of public policies which aggravate the situations with which they are designed to deal. Such policies and many others, such as the cartelization of surface freight transportation,[9] for example, have in common the fact that they are self-perpetuating because they misallocate resources in such fashion as to make people dependent on the misallocation for income. The ConRail system promises to do this in a massive way, partly because of the extra protection it would give the unionized labor force, partly because of its perpetuation of the present technology, and partly because of its perpetuation of the present economic organization of transportation. The present organization of transportation generates a great deal of human capital, in the form of knowledge of how the cartel works, in the possession of lawyers, engineers, traffic men and academic observers, capital which the holders do not wish to have destroyed by an appropriate organization of the industry. Accordingly, ConRail will assuredly generate its own political support so that the present popular suggestion—that it should be formed and then eradicated by a liquidation—is unlikely to be fulfilled.

Apart from the foregoing considerations, policies which deny a market test and which use public funds to invest in or pay the variable expenses of something which is failing a market test greatly weaken the nation. They require the government's resources to be squandered without end unnecessarily and so interfere with the federal government's ability to do those things only governments can do: ensuring national defense, promoting (and policing) domestic tranquility, building roads, dealing with pollution of air and water, preserving free-roaming wild animals from extinction, financing of elementary education, and the other governmental functions generally accepted as appropriate in a free society.

---

[8] John J. Agria, *College Housing* (Washington, D. C.: American Enterprise Institute for Public Policy Research, 1972). The argument presented here is my own, with considerable debt to Professors Armen Alchian and Stanley Warner. Professor Agria concludes the dormitory loan program is undesirable, but on other grounds, notably those of equity between day students and residential students and of biases in choice of expenditures by administrators.

[9] Thomas Gale Moore, *Freight Transportation Regulation* (Washington, D. C.: American Enterprise Institute for Public Policy Research, 1972).

APPENDIX

The tables in this appendix document the decline of the railroads relative to rival carriers since 1960 and the decline of the eastern railroads relative to the railroad industry in the same period.

There is reason to believe that both sets of data understate the declines. Paul M. Zeis, director of research of the Norfolk & Western Railway, argues that tonnages of private carriage and owner-driver common carriage are underestimated in conventional data and suggests that truck ton-miles may actually exceed rail.[1] Tonnage data at best understate the decline of the railroads; rail revenues have gone from 24.2 percent of highway revenues in 1962 to 14.6 percent in 1972. (See Table 2.)

The data on the tonnage and earnings of the eastern railroads relative to all other railroads are biased by the inclusion of the Pocahontas carriers, which originate most of the bituminous coal in West Virginia. Performance of the railroads in the Middle Atlantic and New England regions alone would be much more unfavorable.

---

[1] See "We Don't Have 39 Percent?" *Trains*, March 1975, p. 10.

Table A-1: U.S. INTERCITY FREIGHT BY MODES * (INCLUDING MAIL & EXPRESS)
(billions of ton-miles)

	Rail		Truck		Oil Pipeline		Great Lakes		Rivers and Canals		Air		Total
	Amount	%	Amount	%	Amount	%	Amount	%	Amount	%	Amount	%	
1939	339	62.3	53	9.7	56	10.3	76	14.0	20	3.7	.01	.00	544
1960	579	44.1	285	21.8	229	17.4	99	7.5	121	9.2	.89	.07	1,314
1961	570	43.5	296	22.7	233	17.8	87	6.6	123	9.4	1.01	.08	1,310
1962	600	43.8	309	22.5	238	17.3	90	6.6	133	9.7	1.30	.09	1,371
1963	629	43.3	336	23.1	253	17.4	95	6.5	139	9.6	1.30	.09	1,453
1964	666	43.2	356	23.1	269	17.4	106	6.9	144	9.3	1.50	.10	1,543
1965	709	43.3	359	21.9	306	18.7	110	6.7	152	9.3	1.91	.12	1,638
1966	751	43.0	381	21.8	333	19.1	116	6.6	164	9.4	2.25	.13	1,747
1967	731	41.4	389	22.0	361	20.5	107	6.1	174	9.9	2.59	.15	1,765
1968	757	41.2	396	21.5	391	21.3	112	6.1	179	9.7	2.90	.16	1,838
1969	774	40.8	404	21.3	411	21.7	115	6.1	188	9.9	3.20	.17	1,895
1970	771	39.7	412	21.3	431	22.3	114	5.9	205	10.6	3.30	.17	1,936
1971	746	38.2	445	22.8	444	22.7	105	5.4	210	10.7	3.50	.18	1,954
1972	784	37.7	470	22.7	476	23.0	109	5.3	230	11.1	3.70	.18	2,073
1973	858	38.5	505	22.6	507	22.7	126	5.6	232	10.4	3.94	.18	2,232
1974 (p)	861	38.6	510	22.9	507	22.7	113	5.1	234	10.5	3.60	.16	2,229

* Includes both for-hire and private carriers.
(p) Preliminary.
Source: Transportation Association of America, *Facts and Trends*, 11th ed. (1974), p. 8 (updated).

Table A-2: ESTIMATED UNITED STATES FREIGHT BILL *
($ millions)

	1962	1963	1964	1965	1966	1967	1968	1969	1970	1971	1972	1973
Highway												
Truck—Intercity												
ICC-Regulated	8,131	8,548	9,155	10,068	10,862	11,308	12,715	13,944	14,585	16,700	18,700	21,000
Non-ICC Regulated	12,332	13,040	14,412	13,560	15,698	17,622	17,321	17,439	18,968	20,849	22,990	25,515
Truck—Local	16,536	18,398	20,289	23,041	22,929	24,507	27,852	30,429	35,531	41,622	50,261	57,303
Bus	52	57	63	70	75	84	97	108	122	125	132	137
	37,051	40,043	43,919	46,739	49,564	53,521	57,985	61,920	69,206	79,296	92,083	103,955
Rail												
Railroads	8,960	9,121	9,457	9,923	10,386	10,148	10,685	11,289	11,869	12,730	13,105	14,801
Water												
International	1,526	1,674	1,838	2,081	2,490	2,631	2,917	2,989	3,187	3,195	3,524	4,035
Coastal, Intercoastal	726	716	711	692	704	693	683	692	834	825	844	828
Inland Waterways	323	333	353	381	384	370	425	413	473	547	582	650
Great Lakes	185	190	204	213	227	210	210	237	239	222	243	286
Locks, Channels, etc.	303	315	333	391	393	401	373	350	376	385	417	425
	3,063	3,228	3,439	3,758	4,198	4,305	4,608	4,681	5,109	5,174	5,610	6,224
Oil Pipe Line												
ICC-Regulated	811	840	865	904	941	995	1,023	1,103	1,188	1,249	1,338	1,446
Non-ICC Regulated	128	140	148	147	155	162	182	206	208	243	245	255
	939	980	1,013	1,051	1,096	1,157	1,205	1,309	1,396	1,492	1,583	1,701
Air												
Domestic	311	320	360	428	490	543	593	748	720	759	849	980
International	192	198	223	280	446	520	507	466	451	539	629	611
	503	518	583	708	936	1,063	1,100	1,214	1,171	1,298	1,478	1,591

Table A-2 (continued)

	1962	1963	1964	1965	1966	1967	1968	1969	1970	1971	1972	1973
Other Carriers												
Forwarders & REA Express	418	424	452	470	505	506	492	478	358	330	349	444
Other Shipper Costs												
Loading & Unloading Freight Cars	1,081	1,094	1,104	1,106	1,126	1,076	1,081	1,087	1,059	1,060	1,132	1,232
Operation of Traffic Departments	258	272	284	293	305	316	337	357	374	397	422	448
	1,339	1,366	1,388	1,399	1,431	1,392	1,418	1,444	1,433	1,457	1,554	1,680
GRAND TOTAL	52,273	55,680	60,251	64,048	68,116	72,092	77,493	82,335	90,542	101,777	115,762	130,396
GROSS NATIONAL PRODUCT (billions of dollars)	560.3	590.5	632.4	684.9	749.9	793.9	864.2	930.3	977.1	1,054.9	1,158.0	1,294.9
GRAND TOTAL % OF GNP	9.33	9.43	9.53	9.35	9.08	9.08	8.97	8.85	9.27	9.65	10.00	10.07

* Includes mail and express.

Source: Transportation Association of America, *Facts and Trends*, 11th ed. (1974), p. 4 (updated).

Table A-3: RETURN ON CAPITAL FOR U.S. RAILROADS

Year	United States	Eastern District	Southern District	Western District
1929	5.30%	6.03%	4.27%	4.85%
1939	2.56	3.14	2.77	1.85
1960	2.13	1.55	2.97	2.40
1961	1.97	0.89	3.19	2.58
1962	2.74	1.80	4.17	3.15
1963	3.12	2.28	4.04	3.60
1964	3.16	2.56	4.01	3.43
1965	3.69	3.32	4.16	3.87
1966	3.90	3.55	4.45	4.03
1967	2.46	1.58	3.86	2.75
1968	2.44	1.27	3.79	3.01
1969	2.36	1.10	4.17	2.81
1970	1.73	def.	4.50	3.02
1971	2.47	def.	4.93	3.90
1972	2.96	0.37	5.32	4.24
1973	3.05	0.48	5.46	4.22
1974	3.45	1.12	5.70	4.40

Source: Association of American Railroads, *Yearbook of Railroad Facts* (1975), p. 20.

Table A-4: NET OPERATING INCOME FOR U.S. RAILROADS
($ thousands)

Year	United States	Eastern District	Southern District	Western District
1960	584,016	176,742	113,353	293,921
1961	537,771	99,584	122,641	315,546
1962	725,679	196,571	157,884	371,224
1963	805,658	242,878	152,445	410,336
1964	818,213	270,381	155,416	392,416
1965	961,516	351,197	164,246	446,072
1966	1,045,863	384,574	183,191	478,098
1967	676,434	174,627	164,284	337,523
1968	677,623	139,690	164,445	373,489
1969	654,670	118,700	185,102	350,868
1970	485,854	(101,603)	207,750	379,707
1971	695,539	(32,294)	236,411	491,422
1972	827,685	38,638	258,763	530,285
1973	849,261	50,054	269,760	529,447
1974	981,432	115,308	296,142	569,982

(Parentheses indicate deficit.)
Source: Association of American Railroads, *Yearbook of Railroad Facts* (1975), p. 19.

Table A-5: FREIGHT CAR MILES FOR U.S. RAILROADS
(car-miles in millions)

Year	United States	Eastern District	Southern District	Western District
1960	28,170	9,966	4,207	13,997
1961	27,226	9,451	4,121	13,653
1962	27,772	9,680	4,333	13,759
1963	28,153	9,807	4,418	13,927
1964	28,912	10,033	4,549	14,330
1965	29,336	10,291	4,667	14,378
1966	30,374	10,295	4,950	15,129
1967	29,661	10,104	4,925	14,632
1968	30,082	10,004	4,892	15,187
1969	30,349	9,790	5,125	15,433
1970	29,890	9,505	5,143	15,242
1971	29,181	8,730	5,284	15,166
1972	30,309	8,786	5,623	15,900
1973	31,248	8,796	5,692	16,760
1974	30,729	8,723	5,631	16,375

Source: Association of American Railroads, *Yearbook of Railroad Facts* (1975), p. 38.

Table A-6: ORIGINATED TONNAGE FOR U.S. RAILROADS
(tonnage in thousands)

Year	United States	Eastern District	Southern District	Western District
1960	1,240,654	512,380	250,293	477,981
1961	1,193,740	485,259	247,968	460,513
1962	1,233,597	508,556	259,562	465,479
1963	1,284,848	536,541	272,137	476,170
1964	1,354,612	565,697	285,887	503,028
1965	1,387,423	578,215	297,550	511,658
1966	1,448,901	585,072	313,487	550,342
1967	1,407,628	568,083	328,863	510,682
1968	1,431,308	574,446	330,215	526,647
1969	1,473,457	572,350	340,731	560,376
1970	1,484,919	557,994	351,142	575,784
1971	1,390,960	495,485	348,216	547,260
1972	1,447,864	507,346	367,405	573,113
1973	1,532,165	527,279	380,245	624,641
1974	1,543,300	536,600	387,500	619,200

Source: Association of American Railroads, *Yearbook of Railroad Facts* (1975), p. 28.

Table A-7: FREIGHT TRAIN MILES FOR U.S. RAILROADS
(train-miles in thousands)

Year	United States	Eastern District	Southern District	Western District
1960	404,464	139,979	60,221	204,264
1961	386,410	131,505	58,420	196,485
1962	393,346	133,868	61,152	198,325
1963	399,897	135,783	63,442	200,672
1964	414,470	140,838	65,191	208,440
1965	420,962	142,714	65,652	212,595
1966	437,491	141,828	68,412	227,250
1967	420,365	134,916	67,798	217,651
1968	429,276	134,665	69,448	225,162
1969	433,371	132,691	71,576	229,104
1970	427,065	131,134	74,962	220,969
1971	429,530	128,392	76,892	224,246
1972	451,032	129,601	81,098	240,333
1973	469,122	132,542	82,810	253,770
1974	469,728	128,160	84,391	257,177

Source: Association of American Railroads, *Yearbook of Railroad Facts* (1975), p. 37.

Table A-8: REVENUE TON MILES FOR U.S. RAILROADS
(ton-miles in millions)

Year	United States	Eastern District	Southern District	Western District
1960	572,309	217,731	87,691	266,887
1961	563,361	208,550	87,873	266,938
1962	592,862	220,216	95,829	276,818
1963	621,737	230,382	102,532	288,823
1964	658,639	244,691	108,316	305,631
1965	697,878	259,477	116,836	321,564
1966	738,395	265,504	125,462	347,429
1967	719,498	258,361	127,988	333,149
1968	744,023	259,391	130,686	353,946
1969	767,841	259,827	139,256	368,757
1970	764,809	254,467	140,034	370,309
1971	739,743	225,619	139,660	374,464
1972	776,746	231,221	147,116	398,410
1973	851,809	245,022	157,879	448,907
1974	853,887	248,543	160,828	444,517

Source: Association of American Railroads, *Yearbook of Railroad Facts* (1975), p. 29.

Cover and book design: Pat Taylor

THE NORTHEAST
RAILROAD PROBLEM